Spiritual Training Manual

Holy Spirit Led Ministries
#1 Healing Ministriy in the Midwest David & Patricia Lage
Co-Founders
HolySpiritLedMinistries@gmail.com
www.HSLM.us " I Believe in Miracles" Mondays 7-8 pm
Our facebook group Holy Spirt Led Ministries

Written by Michael Politoski

Copyright 2017

www.spiritualfirstresponders.com

Spiritual First Responder Training Manual

Copyright ©2017 Michael Politoski

All rights reserved under international Copyright law. Contents and / or cover may not be reproduced in whole or in part in any form without the express written permission of the publisher.

Published by: Spiritual First Responders, Inc.

Printed in the United States of America

ISBN-13:
978-1977826169

ISBN-10:
1977826164

Spiritual First Responders, Inc.
118 S. Church Street
Asheboro, NC 27203
USA

Email: info@spiritualfirstresponders.com
Website: www.spiritualfirstresponders.com

Scripture taken from the New King James Version®. Copyright © 1982 by Thomas Nelson, Inc. Used by permission. All rights reserved.

Dedication

Where would you be today if it weren't for friends that knew how to pray for you during difficult times? This book is dedicated to two such friends of mine, prayer warriors Reverend Raymond Mitchell, and his dear wife, Reverend Alla Mitchell. During the darkest time of my life, they were beacons of light for me, praying the Prayer of Faith over me in a hospital room after cancer surgery. It is through their efforts that the power of Divine Healing became real to me. I have committed my life to service in healing ministry, because they showed me that Jesus still heals today.

I would also like to say thanks to a few of the other people in my life who have helped me gain a better understanding of the principles of Divine Healing. It has been said that iron sharpens iron, and over the countless hours of research into this fascinating field of study, many spirited conversations were held with these men of God. So, to my brothers in Christ, Pat Rutherford, Dave Lage, and Andy Hayner, thank you for being there for me.

Most importantly, on this side of Heaven at least, I want to thank my dear wife Letty for standing by me during the difficult times we have seen. Her tireless willingness to work when I could not, her strong belief in our marital vows, and her prayers have helped make the material presented in these pages possible. She stood by me when the situation looked hopeless; she fought for me when I could not. A wonderful mother, wife, and best friend, Letty I love you and thank you for who you are.

Spiritual First Responder Training Manual

Table of Contents

	Dedication	3
	Introduction	7
1	The Word of God	9
2	Your Relationship with Jesus Christ	17
3	The Incredible Grace of God	29
4	The Power of the Holy Spirit	41
5	Your Spiritual Identity	53
6	The Believer's Authority	63
7	Traditions of Men	73
8	Healing the Sick	81
9	Healing Techniques	97
10	Maintaining Your Healing	115
	About the Author	121

Introduction

How exciting it is to learn that Jesus still miraculously heals people today! Incredibly, most people are unaware of this amazing fact. The Bible is very clear about our obligations to carry on the ministry of Jesus Christ through the laying on of hands for the purposes of ministering healing.

Becoming a Spiritual First Responder assures that you have the proper training to handle spiritual situations that you will encounter. In the pages of this manual, you will learn the facts about Divine Healing, and how to use it as a tool to promote the Gospel.

Healing techniques are discussed; what works best, and what can actually hinder your healing ministry. You will learn about your identity in Christ, the power of the Believer's Authority and how you can be used of Jesus to see miracles manifest before your very eyes!

Working for the Kingdom of God is exciting. This course will strengthen your faith, and boost your confidence. You will go forth and lay hands on the sick, seeing them recover. Enjoy the journey…

Special Note

The author and publisher of this manual and any associated materials are in no way trained medical professionals or psychological professionals. The material presented herein is for historical information only. Any reference to instruction or practices is in no way to be construed as medical advice. If you are sick, please seek attention from a trained medical physician or organization immediately.

Chapter 1

The Word of God

In order to become an effective Spiritual First Responder, it is important to have a strong Biblical foundation on which your beliefs are based. Without this basic understanding, your results will likely be limited. There is power revealed in the true Word of God, and it is available to you as a believer in your quest to help others.

As you begin your journey to becoming a Spiritual First Responder, please note that it is not necessary to have an exhaustive, complete theological background to have an effective ministry. If you decide to wait until you understand the Bible from cover to cover before you begin practicing the techniques presented here, you may never see the miracles that await you. Do not fall into the trap of believing that you are not smart enough to understand how healing works, as Jesus has made it quite simple. There are basic beliefs that come into play, and with these beliefs, you can move mountains.

First and foremost, it is imperative that you understand exactly what the Bible is, and what it contains. This may seem elementary to most Christians, but since what we are called to do is so important, we will take nothing for granted. When you come to realize the awesome truths in the Bible, it will transform your complete outlook on life. Its pages contain wisdom, truth, and power.

It took about 1600 years to write the Bible, spanning a time period from 1500 BC to AD 100. It was written by approximately forty men, all inspired by the Holy Spirit.

Originally written in Hebrew, Aramaic, and Greek, the Bible has now been translated into over twelve-hundred languages, including several different English translations, or versions, of the Bible. It routinely shows up on many bestseller lists, and reliable sources estimate approximately 100 million Bibles are sold, or given away every year.

There are many books written about and by various religions, however the Bible is the only one which can correctly claim to contain the actual words of God. Spiritual First Responders believe that God inspired various authors through the years to write down His actual words for us.

The Bible is considered to be one book, but actually it contains sixty-six smaller books. The Bible is divided into two parts, the Old Testament, and the New Testament. This amazing book documents history before the birth of Jesus Christ, along with His life and ministry, and beyond.

The Old Covenant is mainly found in the Old Testament. It was a covenant between God and the Children of Israel, the Jews. It included a set of laws that required strict adherence, evoking the wrath of God for those who disobeyed it. Priests offered animal sacrifices for the atonement of sins, as a shadow or foretelling of things to come through Jesus.

The New Covenant is found in the New Testament and extends to the Jews. When Jesus came to Earth to destroy the works of the devil, He became the ultimate sacrifice for all of man's sins, and God placed all wrath and judgment on Him at the cross. Jesus forever restored man's fellowship with God. The New Covenant and its promises extend God's grace to us as believers. Living under grace frees us from the constraints of the laws in the Old Testament.

Romans 3:20-24

"Therefore by the deeds of the law no flesh will be justified in His sight, for by the law is the knowledge of sin. But now the righteousness of God apart from the law is revealed, being witnessed by the Law and the Prophets, even the righteousness of God, through faith in Jesus Christ, to all and on all who believe. For there is no difference; for all have sinned and fall short of the glory of God, being justified freely by His grace through the redemption that is in Christ Jesus."

The Bible is the written Word of God. It is true down to the very last detail. The Word of God has been here since the very beginning of time, and Jesus is the physical manifestation of the Word. Many believe the Bible is a collection of stories and fairy tales, no longer applicable to the standards of today. Yes, the Bible contains stories that were documented and written by men, but they were inspired by the Holy Spirit. When you see a promise in the Bible, and we will cover many, you can absolutely stand on the truth presented in it.

Sadly, man's misinterpretation of the Bible, if believed, can sometimes render you less effective in your duties as a Spiritual First Responder. Therefore, it is important to always go to the written Word for your reference, and avoid these long-held traditions of men that are being taught in many churches today. Any teaching that says healing is not for today is inaccurate, and unscriptural. Though hard to believe, these teachings can hinder the Word of God. Just remember it only dilutes the power of the people who sit under such teachings, and does not globally affect the power of God.

Mark 7:13

"Making the Word of God of no effect through your tradition which you have handed down. And many such things you do."

There are no contradictions in the Bible. Sometimes various people claim to find inconsistencies, but they have to take verses out of context to do so. When looking at the Bible as a whole and understanding its teachings, there are no contradictions. Of equal importance, it is not recommended to form a doctrine over any single verse in the Bible. To be rightly divided, the subject matter needs to be discussed at least twice in the Bible before considering that particular subject to possibly be viewed as a doctrine.

The Bible is not complicated, and there should be no hesitation on your part to open it up and explore its contents. As a Spiritual First Responder, your main focus will be the study of the ministry of Jesus, found in the New Testament. As you begin to read about the events in His life, ask the Holy Spirit to reveal the truth to you. After all, the Holy Spirit wrote the Bible, and He will help it to come alive so you can see it manifest in your life.

As you begin to learn more about the Bible, you will realize the price Jesus paid for redemption of your sins, healing for your body, and provision for your life. Understanding the differences between the Old Covenant, mainly found in the Old Testament, and the New Covenant which is in the New Testament, is a key benefit to operating in power, delegated to you by Jesus. Through His name, as evidenced in the true Word of God, you are authorized to heal the sick, cast out demons, raise the dead, preach and teach, and to do all other things which Jesus accomplished in His ministry while on Earth, and even greater things as foretold by Him.

John 14:12

"Most assuredly, I say to you, he who believes in Me, the works that I do he will do also; and greater works than these he will do because I go to My Father."

You must believe the Word of God is true from cover to cover, though you do not have to understand it all to become an effective healing minister.

As written in the Word of God, Jesus has delegated His authority to us as Spiritual First Responders since we are believers, commanding us to heal the sick.

Matthew 28:18-19

"And Jesus spoke to them, saying, 'All authority has been given to me in Heaven and on Earth. Go therefore and make disciples of all nations, baptizing them in the name of the Father and of the Son and of the Holy Spirit.'"

His Word is timeless; God's Word is eternal.

Matthew 24:35

"Heaven and Earth will pass away, but My words will by no means pass away."

The Holy Spirit inspired the Bible. Additionally, the Word of God was here since the beginning of time. Jesus is the physical manifestation of the Word of God.

2 Timothy 3:16-17

"All Scripture is given by inspiration of God, and is profitable for doctrine, for reproof, for correction, for instruction in righteousness, that the man of God may be thoroughly equipped for every good work."

John 1:1-2

"In the beginning was the Word, and the Word was with God, and the Word was God. He was in the beginning with God."

1 John 5:6-7

"This is He who came by water and blood – Jesus Christ; not only by water, but by water and blood. And it is the Spirit who bears witness, because the Spirit is truth. For there are three that bear witness in Heaven: the Father, the Word, and the Holy Spirit; and these three are one."

Do not be afraid to explore the Word of God. Devour its contents, and feed on it. The Bible contains every answer to life's challenges.

In summary, the Bible is truth. Learn from it, and trust in it.

Here are some additional, important scriptures for your reference:

Psalm 119:105

"Thy Word is a lamp unto my feet and a light to my path."

Isaiah 55:11

"So shall my Word be that goes forth from my mouth; it shall not return to me void, but it shall accomplish what I please, and it shall prosper in the thing for which I sent it."

Psalm 107:20

"He sent His Word and healed them, and delivered them from their destructions."

Psalm 119:11

"Your Word have I hid in my heart, that I might not sin against You."

Romans 10:17

"So then faith comes by hearing, and hearing by the word of God."

Include your favorite scriptures here:

Chapter 2

Your Relationship with Jesus Christ

Probably the most important thing to consider when becoming a Spiritual First Responder is your personal relationship with Jesus Christ. There is a huge difference in the knowledge of Jesus Christ, and a relationship with Him. Just knowing that Jesus existed, or that He is the Son of God is not enough. The Bible says that even the demons know this to be true. The demons are aware of the existence and power of Jesus. Simply knowing the facts surrounding His genealogy, teachings, and Divinity are not enough to prove the existence of a relationship with Him. Yes, even the demons are aware of who Jesus is:

Mark 1:23-24

"Now there was a man in their synagogue with an unclean spirit. And he cried out, saying, 'Let us alone! What have we to do with You, Jesus of Nazareth? I know who you are – the Holy One of God!'"

Many people are under the false assumption that being baptized as a child, or regular church attendance validates a relationship with Jesus. Or, perhaps their parents were religious, or their upbringing was godly, or they are trying to live a good life, and that means they love Jesus. Maybe, at one point, they even said a prayer that sounded very important to them. Obviously, these things have merit, but they do not necessarily constitute a personal relationship with Jesus. Being a good person and being generous and nice are good qualities, but do you love Jesus? Have you made Him Lord of your life? You can live a good life, help the poor, sing in the church choir, read the Bible all you want and still miss the whole point of knowing and trusting a loving Jesus with your life here on Earth, and in the life to come in Heaven. Tragically, many church members and seemingly religious people will not be found walking the streets of Heaven.

Other things that people routinely use as proof to justify a relationship with Jesus are: The keeping of the Ten Commandments, regular church attendance, tithing, and observing religious traditions. Again, these are typical actions that people point to when they claim to be a follower of Christ. Practicing religion is no substitute for knowing Jesus Christ. The Bible speaks to this as having a form of Godliness, but denying the power thereof:

2 Timothy 3:5

"Having a form of godliness but denying its power. And from such people turn away!"

The above listed actions may very well happen if you have a relationship with Jesus, but never depend on your works or good behavior to get you to Heaven. Jesus is the only way.

John 14:6

"Jesus said to him, 'I am the way, the truth, and the life. No one comes to the Father except through me.'"

Probably the most recognized verse of all time is found in the book of John:

John 3:16

"For God so loved the world that He gave His only begotten Son, that whoever believes in Him should not perish but have eternal life."

Romans 5:8

"But God demonstrates His own love toward us, in that while we were still sinners, Christ died for us."

Your works alone are not enough to get you to Heaven or to enjoy the benefits of the Kingdom of God while living here on Earth. Only Jesus can make this possible for you. Jesus plus anything else is more than you need. He paid the price for you.

In the old days, living under the Old Covenant, the priests had to make sacrifices of animals for the atonement of man's sins. This process was repeated over and over for hundreds of years until God sent Jesus to be the ultimate sacrifice for all of our sins, once and for all. Born of the Virgin Mary, He was the spotless, sinless, sacrifice that was needed to reclaim man's dominion over the Earth, destroying the works of Satan, who had cheated Adam and Eve out of their authority through deceit.

The devil actually used misinterpretation of God's Word to confuse Adam and Eve, causing the fall of mankind to happen. At that point in time, sin entered into man's bloodline, and the dominion of the Earth was surrendered to Satan. For about two-thousand years, man lived under the grace of God until sin became rampant. At this time, God delivered the law to Moses, and began to judge sin. The law was not given to make man righteous, but it was there to bring about the consciousness of sin, and the eventual need for a lasting sacrifice to atone for our sins. The Old Testament is full of prophecies about the coming Messiah:

Isaiah 7:14

"Therefore the Lord Himself will give you a sign: Behold the virgin shall conceive and bear a Son, and shall call His name Immanuel."

Jesus, the Living Word of God, born of the Virgin Mary arrived on the scene with little fanfare, being born in a stable used to house animals. From the Gospels, we can garner plenty of details about His birth, but there is very little information about His childhood. There is much speculation about what Jesus did as a child, but it suffices to say that He, like other Jewish children of the day, studied the scriptures at length. At the age of twelve, He was found in the Temple discussing scriptures with those present:

Luke 2:46-47

"Now so it was that after three days they found Him in the temple, sitting in the midst of the teachers, both listening to them and asking them questions. And all who heard Him were astonished at His understanding and answers."

Jesus came to the Earth as a man, having to go through the same challenges that we all face growing up. He learned to walk and talk, studied the scriptures, and was the son of a carpenter. At the age of thirty, he was baptized by John the Baptist, indwelled by the Holy Spirit, and began His ministry of three years preaching and teaching about the

Kingdom of God through demonstration of power by casting out demons, healing the sick, and raising the dead. All that met Him were amazed by His teachings, and His vast insight into the things of God.

Matthew 3:16-17

"When He had been baptized, Jesus came up immediately from the water; and behold the heavens were opened to Him, and He saw the Spirit of God descending like a dove and alighting upon Him. And suddenly a voice came from Heaven, saying, 'This is My beloved Son, in whom I am well pleased.'"

Jesus then went into the wilderness and was tempted by Satan, after which he began His teachings about the Kingdom of Heaven.

Matthew 4:17

"From that time Jesus began to preach and to say, 'Repent for the Kingdom of Heaven is at hand.'"

Jesus came to Earth for a specific mission. If you ask, most people will claim that He came to die for the redemption of our sins. The stated mission of Jesus Christ in the Word of God accomplishes that, but there's more:

1 John 3:8

"He who sins is of the devil, for the devil has sinned from the beginning. For this purpose the Son of God was manifested, that He might destroy the works of the devil."

Satan had stolen the fellowship of man with God through the injection of sin into society. Satan is the author of death:

Hebrews 2:14-15

"Inasmuch then as the children have partaken of flesh and blood, He Himself likewise shared in the same, that through death He might destroy him who had the power of death, that is, the devil."

Jesus came to destroy the works of the enemy!

Matthew 10:34

"Do not think that I came to bring peace on Earth. I did not come to bring peace but a sword."

Jesus came to restore the fellowship between God and man, destroying the constraints of the law, and reconciling all sin unto Himself so that God's wrath toward man should cease for all those who believe in Jesus.

Yes, He died for our sins, but this was a necessity for our salvation through the grace of God. His purpose was to restore man's dominion on Earth, and forever restore the intimate relationship between God and man. He was beaten for our healing; He was crucified for the redemption of our sins. He arose on the third day taking back the keys of death from Satan, and affording us everlasting life.

Not everyone was happy with the teachings of Jesus. Not everyone will be happy with the duties you perform as a Spiritual First Responder either. The religious people of His time accused Jesus of blasphemy, and sought to put Him to death for it. They even accused Jesus of healing in the name of the devil, and it is not uncommon for people to do the same today. A personal relationship with Jesus comes with many benefits, but be ready to defend your position in Him by knowing what the Word of God says about your adversaries, and how they will attack your efforts to promote the Gospel of Jesus. The Bible says to count it all joy when you encounter such challenges, as it means you are likely on the right path when you see these things.

As prophesied in the Old Testament, Jesus was tried, beaten for our healing, and crucified on the cross, becoming the propitiation for our sins. He conquered death, however, and rose again having taken the keys of death and Hell from Satan, thereby providing eternal life for all who enter into a relationship with Him as Lord and Savior. It is in this death, burial, and resurrection that we receive the power and authority to operate as Spiritual First Responders.

Isaiah 53:4-5

"Surely He has borne our griefs and carried our sorrows; yet we esteemed Him stricken, smitten by God, and afflicted. But He was wounded for our transgressions, He was bruised for our iniquities; the chastisement for our peace was upon Him, and by His stripes we are healed."

Again, confirmed in the New Testament:

1 Peter 2:24

"Who Himself bore our sins in His own body on the tree, that we, having died to sins, might live for righteousness – by whose stripes you were healed."

The knowledge of all discussed so far is helpful, but it does not constitute a relationship with Jesus. We must accept Him as Lord and Savior; we must believe on His name, confess Him with our mouth, and believe that God has raised Him from the dead. Then, the Bible says, we shall be saved.

Romans 10:9

"That if you confess with your mouth the Lord Jesus and believe in your heart that God has raised Him from the dead, you will be saved."

Romans 10:13

"For whoever calls on the name of the Lord shall be saved."

Jesus is the only way to salvation, the only way to God. You are saved by grace, and not by your own works.

John 14:6

"Jesus said to him, 'I am the way, the truth, and the life. No one comes to the Father except through me.'"

Ephesians 2:8-9

"For by grace you have been saved through faith, and not of yourselves; it is the gift of God, not of works, lest anyone should boast."

It takes belief in Him and what He did on our behalf to rescue us from the sin that traps and dooms us to eternal separation from God. In Jesus, you become a new creation.

Jesus is the truth, and the only way to God. There is no other way, no other person, no other deed or work that is going to make it possible. Jesus is the only way. When you come to the point of realizing that you can do nothing without Jesus, but can do anything with Him, and when you confess with your mouth the belief in the death, burial, and resurrection of Jesus, knowing why He did these things, and you honestly believe it to be true in your heart, you have a relationship with Him. Ask Him to be your Lord and Savior, to live in your heart, to forgive you of your sins, and then surrender yourself to Him. Having done this, you are now united with Him as a co-laborer in His mission to destroy the works of the devil and preach the Kingdom of God. This true partnership with Him is evidence of a relationship with Him. Jesus now lives in you and operates through you in continuance of His ministry, just as it was when He walked here on Earth.

Accepting Jesus Christ as your Lord and Savior guarantees that you will go to Heaven when you die. Eternal life, however, starts the moment you accept Jesus as your Savior. This means you are entitled to all the benefits that come with being a child of God. Many see the acceptance of Christ as a ticket to Heaven, avoiding Hell, much like a personal fire insurance policy. Sadly, these new Christians never advance in the knowledge of what their relationship with Christ provides for them. Knowledge is power, and the Bible says that people will perish from lack of it. Yes, they will make it to Heaven, and they might even get there sooner because they fail to realize that it is possible to walk in Divine health, and prosperity, since they are now citizens of the Kingdom of God, here on Earth. We as Christians are joint heirs with Jesus to all the benefits of the Kingdom of

God, and we are encouraged repeatedly in the Bible to immediately take advantage of these provisions.

2 Corinthians 6:2

"For He says: 'In an acceptable time I have heard you, and in the day of salvation I have helped you.' Behold, now is the acceptable time; behold, now is the day of salvation."

Here is a prayer that will help you begin your relationship with Jesus:

"Heavenly Father, I know that I have sinned against You. I know you love me Lord, but I realize that none of my works can save me. I repent of my sins, and turn away from the things I have done in the past. Please forgive me, and help me avoid doing these things again. I believe that your Son, Jesus Christ died for my sins, was resurrected from the dead, is alive, and is ready to save me right now. Jesus, I invite You to become the Lord of my life, and to live in my heart right now. Please send your Holy Spirit to help me serve You, and to do Your will for the rest of my life. In Jesus' name I pray, Amen."

Technically, the sinner's prayer is never mentioned in scripture, but has been adopted as a convenient way to cover the essential steps of confessing Christ, and the need for you to acknowledge your sincere belief in what He has done for the redemption of all your sins. It is not the prayer that saves you, but the belief in what you are saying in this prayer. There is a huge difference between the two.

It is up to us as Christians to propagate the Gospel to others. Tell them of the Good News of Jesus, and what He can do for them. As a Spiritual First Responder, you will be demonstrating the power of God through healing, and you will have ample opportunity to bring new converts into the Kingdom of God. As in the time of Jesus, when miracles happen, people will be amazed and they will want to know how and why these things transpire. The opportunities to preach the love of Jesus will be plentiful, and the responses will be amazing as you lead others to the Lord.

In summary, your relationship with Jesus may indeed begin with a prayer, but don't let it end there. You are immediately empowered to do the works of Jesus the moment you accept Him as your Savior.

Here are some scriptures for you to ponder when considering your relationship with Jesus:

Romans 3:23

"For all have sinned and fall short of the glory of God."

Romans 6:23

"For the wages of sin is death, but the gift of God is eternal life in Christ Jesus our Lord."

Romans 10:9

"That if you confess with your mouth the Lord Jesus and believe in your heart that God has raised Him from the dead, you will be saved."

Romans 10:13

"For whoever calls on the name of the Lord shall be saved."

Matthew 28:18-19

"And Jesus spoke to them, saying, 'All authority has been given to me in Heaven and on Earth. Go therefore and make disciples of all nations, baptizing them in the name of the Father and of the Son and of the Holy Spirit.'"

Mark 16:17-18

"And these things will follow those who believe: In My name they will cast out demons, they will speak with new tongues, they will take up serpents; and if they drink anything deadly, it will by no means hurt them; they will lay hands on the sick, and they will recover."

Include your favorite scriptures here:

Chapter 3

The Incredible Grace of God

Grace is defined as the free and unmerited favor of God, as manifested in the salvation of sinners and the bestowal of blessings. In other words, though we did not even deserve it, God sent His only Son, Jesus to serve as a sacrifice so that we may experience eternal life and fellowship with God. This total act of selflessness was done on our behalf so we could enjoy a renewed relationship with God the Father.

Clearly, a whole case study could be made about the subject of grace. Without it, we are helpless as Christians. Grace is the key to our salvation, as nothing we can do as humans could ever warrant eternal life in Heaven. We have all sinned and come short of the glory of God.

Romans 3:23

"For all have sinned and fall short of the glory of God."

The Christian life, or relationship with Jesus, relies on two things: What God has already done, and what we must do.

We will examine our part later, but notice what God has done for us. The Bible says that while we were yet sinners, Christ died for us:

Romans 5:8

"But God demonstrates His own love toward us, in that while we were still sinners, Christ died for us."

The Bible says that all have sinned, and that none of us are worthy, in and of ourselves, to merit such salvation. By grace we are saved, and not through any works of our own, lest we should boast.

Ephesians 2:8-9

"For by grace you have been saved through faith, and not of yourselves; it is the gift of God, not of works, lest anyone should boast."

The bottom line is that God loved us so much, that He took on the form of a man, Christ Jesus, and paid the ultimate price for the restoration of man's dominion over the Earth, and a renewed relationship with Himself. In the beginning, Adam and Eve enjoyed this communion with God, but surrendered their Earthly dominion to Satan through a simple act of disobedience.

For nearly two-thousand years, God allowed His relationship with man to be covered under grace. However, man took advantage of this, and sin began to run rampant, and unchecked. At this point, God delivered the law and the Ten Commandments to Moses, which included severe penalties for those who violated them. In a sense, the law was given to help people become aware, or conscious of their sins. No one could adhere to the strict standards of the law, which created the knowledge of the need for atonement to purge the sins and seek forgiveness. Priests would routinely perform animal sacrifices, shedding innocent blood, to obtain forgiveness of sin. Thus, the Old Covenant was in place for this purpose. The Old Testament prophets began to testify about the coming Messiah, Jesus, as the ultimate sacrifice that would take away all the sins of the world.

The Word of God is truth, and as prophesied, Jesus came to Earth for such a purpose. He did not come to bring peace, but He came to destroy the works of the Devil which had robbed mankind of its intimate relationship with God. He went about preaching and teaching, casting out demons, healing the sick, and raising the dead.

Then came the time for the fulfillment of prophecy; that of His death, burial, and resurrection. Before He was nailed to the cross, He was beaten and scourged at the whipping post. The Bible says He was completely disfigured due to this beating, and that He bore our grief, sorrows, and pain, and by His stripes we are healed. Lifted up on the cross, He shed His precious blood for the redemption of our sins. Then it was finished, with all the fanfare of earthquakes, darkness, and the splitting of the Temple veil which separated man from God, forever eliminating the need for animal sacrifices. Jesus bowed His head, and died. He did not have to do this; He willingly laid down His life for all of humanity, and paid for every sin, past, present, and future. One time, one death, all sins covered in that instant.

We as Christians know the story doesn't end there. On the third day, Jesus arose from the grave defeating forever the sting of death. He took back the keys of death and Hell from Satan. Shortly thereafter, He ascended back up into Heaven where He is seated at the right hand of God the Father.

We are covered by the grace of God. While we were yet sinners, Christ died for us. Those who have accepted Him as Lord and Savior are forever covered by this grace. There is nothing we can do that will separate us from the love of God. There is no sin that His blood did not cover, even sins that you may commit in the future. He has forgiven your sins, and He loves you more than anything.

Whereas the law of the Old Testament causes us to think about sin and the wrath of God, the life of Jesus causes us to think about the love of God and His total forgiveness of our sins and the complete restoration of our fellowship with Him. This is the New Covenant, the covering of our sins by the grace of God.

The book of Romans is great material to study because it lets us know the difference of living under the law, and under the promises of the New Covenant, through Jesus.

Under the law, if you are guilty of breaking any law, you are guilty of breaking them all. The law was impossible to keep, and this is exactly the point God was making when He gave it. The law brought about awareness of sin.

Romans 11:6

"But if it is by grace, it is no longer on the basis of works; otherwise grace is no longer grace."

Romans 6:14

"For sin shall not have dominion over you, for you are not under law but under grace."

Whereas the law causes us to think about sin, and the wages of sin, the grace of God allows us to concentrate on His love for us through Christ Jesus.

Romans 3:20-24

"Therefore by the deeds of the law no flesh will be justified in His sight, for by the law is the knowledge of sin. But now the righteousness of God apart from the law is revealed, being witnessed by the Law and the Prophets, even the righteousness of God, through faith in Jesus Christ, to all and on all who believe. For there is no difference; for all have sinned and fall short of the glory of God, being justified freely by His grace through the redemption that is in Christ Jesus."

Jesus came to Earth to destroy the works of the devil. A sinless, spotless sacrifice that forever satisfied the requirements for the atonement of sin, he was beaten, crucified, and resurrected thereby reclaiming eternal life and redemption of sins for mankind. Fellowship between God and man had to be restored, and Jesus accomplished this.

Jesus has done His part. God has done His part by extending grace to us, no longer imputing our sins against us. Jesus died for the sins of the world, past, present and future sins, all of them.

What is our part? We know what God has done, what must we do to take advantage of this grace? While it is true that God's grace covers all sin, not everyone accepts this offer from Him, and they reject Jesus and the price He paid to redeem them. We simply need to accept His generous offer.

We must exercise faith, and belief that this is real. We must place our trust in Jesus as Savior and Lord. It is not enough to have head knowledge of this; we must accept it as truth. It is by grace that we are saved, and not of works. Jesus plus any other requirement is more than you need. Nothing you can do in and of yourself could ever warrant such a blessing; it is a gift of God. The Word is clear, it is a gift.

Romans 11:6

"But if it is by grace, it is no longer on the basis of works, otherwise grace is no longer grace."

What this means is simple. You must have total trust in what Jesus did, and total acceptance of the grace God makes available. Faith is the bridge between mankind and God. Jesus is the only way, and belief in Him is the only requirement for us to take advantage of this grace.

John 3:16

"For God so loved the world that He gave His only begotten Son, that whoever believes in Him should not perish but have eternal life."

Many denominations try to add to the equation, attempting to have us live under bits and pieces of the old law. Often stating that we must not wear makeup or jewelry, we must observe the Sabbath, knock on doors handing out tracts, or we must go to church several times weekly; these regulations are burdensome, and totally unscriptural. If you focus on the law, or feel you have to do certain things to merit God's favor, you are cheapening the death of Jesus Christ and the total price He paid for our freedoms. There is nothing that we as humans could ever do that would merit His favor, and that is the beauty of grace.

Galatians 2:16

"Knowing that a man is not justified by the works of the law but by faith in Jesus Christ, even we have believed in Christ Jesus, that we might be justified by faith in Christ and not by the works of the law; for by the works of the law no flesh shall be justified."

If you are asked to obey bits and pieces of the law in order to obtain salvation or God's grace, the Bible says you are making the death of Jesus to be inconsequential:

Galatians 2:21

"I do not set aside the grace of God; for if righteousness comes through the law, then Christ died in vain."

If you realize the grace of God, you know that He loves you, and gives you the freedom to live without the constraints of the old law. The Bible states, if you love Him, you will automatically seek to keep His commandments, but you are not bound by them. You live under grace, the grace of God.

God is not sitting in Heaven with a giant scorecard keeping track of every good or bad deed you are doing. When He looks upon us, He sees our spirit which is made perfect in Jesus Christ. He overlooks our sins because Jesus has already made atonement for every one of them, even ones that we will commit in the future.

Romans 4:8

"Blessed is the man to whom the Lord shall not impute sin."

Alternatively, grace does not give you a free license to sin. If you do sin, God still loves you, and His provisions for you are still available. However, sin has its consequences. Sin opens up your life to attacks from Satan, including disease and disaster. We live in a fallen world; the wages of sin are death, but God's gift is eternal life. We should never consider the calamity in our life as being the wrath or judgment of God. It isn't, as He placed all of that on Jesus at the cross. Living under grace should cause you to love God in return, thereby repenting and turning away from sin.

Many churches adopt the grace concept as a means to cover abhorrent behavior. God still takes a dim view of the sins mentioned in the Bible. If people are engaging in these sins, it speaks more to the lack of a relationship between them and Jesus. Loving Him will cause you to repent, or turn away, from your sin. Behold He makes all things new, as we put off the old man, and put on the new. We are perfected in our spirits through acceptance of Jesus.

Ephesians 4:21-24

"If indeed you have heard Him and have been taught by Him, as the truth is in Jesus: that you put off, concerning your former conduct, the old man which grows corrupt according to the deceitful lusts, and be renewed in the spirit of your mind, and that you put on the new man which was created according to God, in true righteousness and holiness."

2 Timothy 2:1

"You therefore, my son, be strong in the grace that is in Christ Jesus."

John 14:15

"If you love Me, keep My commandments."

Sin has its consequences. Alcoholism affects your health; sexual sins affect your health. The wages of sin is death. Sin creates the calamity in your life, not God. Avoid any sin that is mentioned in the Bible, as God still hates sin.

Desiring to live a sinless life is proof of your love for Jesus, and what He has done for you. Yes, we will mess up from time to time, just know it is covered. Repent of sin and do your best so that others will see the Jesus in you.

If you are constantly dwelling on sin, and constantly confessing your sins to God, then you are bound by sin consciousness, just as if you were living under the law. Let it go. It is the greatest liar of them all, Satan, that seeks to torture you with this condemnation, not God. Accept the fact that God doesn't look at your sins, therefore neither should you. He chooses to forget your sins, and so should you. Never believe the lie that your past will make you an ineffective minister of the Gospel.

Romans 8:1

"There is therefore now no condemnation to those who are in Christ Jesus, who do not walk according to the flesh, but according to the spirit."

Finally, under God's grace, we are free from His wrath and judgment. He placed His entire wrath on Jesus. Contrary to what many doctrines teach, God does not inflict disease or calamity on us in an effort to get us on the right track, or punish us. He would no more do this to us than we would do it to our own children. He loved us so much that He sent His only Son to make things right. When we accept Jesus, and believe in what He did for us, we become joint heirs with Him, children of God.

In summary, the gift of God's grace to us is awesome. It best works for us if we fully realize what Jesus' death and resurrection truly mean for us as Christians. Avoid any teachings that attempt to force you to live under the law, or those asking you to add anything to what Jesus has already accomplished. If you have truly repented of your sins, and have a relationship with Jesus, then never let your past dictate what your future holds for you in ministry.

Here are some scriptures for your reference:

Romans 3:20-24

"Therefore by the deeds of the law no flesh will be justified in His sight, for by the law is the knowledge of sin. But now the righteousness of God apart from the law is revealed, being witnessed by the Law and the Prophets, even the righteousness of God, through faith in Jesus Christ, to all and on all who believe. For there is no difference; for all have sinned and fall short of the glory of God, being justified freely by His grace through the redemption that is in Christ Jesus."

Hebrews 4:16

"Let us therefore come boldly to the throne of grace that we may obtain mercy and find grace to help in time of need."

Romans 6:14

"For sin shall not have dominion over you, for you are not under law but under grace."

James 4:6

"But He gives more grace. Therefore He says: 'God resists the proud, but gives grace to the humble.'"

Romans 5:8

"But God demonstrates His own love toward us, in that while we were yet sinners, Christ died for us."

2 Timothy 2:1

"You therefore, my son, be strong in the grace that is in Christ Jesus."

Isaiah 53:4-5

"Surely He has borne our griefs and carried our sorrows; yet we esteemed Him stricken, smitten by God, and afflicted. But He was wounded for our transgressions, He was bruised for our iniquities; the chastisement for our peace was upon Him, and by His stripes we are healed."

Include your favorite scriptures here:

Chapter 4

The Power of the Holy Spirit

As a Spiritual First Responder, you need to have every resource available to you in order to achieve the ultimate mission of helping others. One very important weapon in your arsenal is the power of the Holy Spirit, or Holy Ghost as He is often referred to.

A Spiritual First Responder believes the written Word of God. The Bible is our official instruction manual, and it gives you information about how you are to equip yourself to respond to spiritual emergencies. A person being attacked by disease, or plagued with mental torment from spirits of infirmity, is considered such an emergency.

The Baptism of the Holy Spirit is often a controversial subject amongst various denominations, and many of them teach against it. Some churches even go so far as to claim that speaking in tongues, which is evidence of the Baptism of the Holy Spirit, is actually of the devil. To be perfectly clear, it is not absolutely necessary to have the Baptism of the Holy Spirit to see results in your healing ministry. However, if you want to see more results, it is recommended that you consider asking Jesus for this gift.

Blasphemy of the Holy Spirit is often described as attributing the miracles of Jesus to the power of Satan. This concept is mentioned in the Bible as an unforgivable sin. Shortly after Jesus had ministered to a man in need of physical healing and demonic deliverance, the scribes claimed that Jesus had operated through the power of Satan, thus committing the unforgivable sin of blasphemy of the Holy Spirit:

Mark 3:22, 29

"And the scribes who came down from Jerusalem said, 'He has Beelzebub,' and, 'By the ruler of the demons He casts out demons.' But he who blasphemes against the Holy Spirit never has forgiveness, but is subject to eternal condemnation."

At best, regardless of your education about tongues, it would probably be a good idea to refrain from saying that tongues are of the devil.

When Jesus began His ministry on Earth, the Bible says the Holy Spirit descended on Him like a dove, and indwelled Him giving Him the power to become an effective minister. Though He was God in the flesh, Jesus was still a human being, and having the Holy Spirit in Him was a clear example of how we should proceed in our ministry. If you want to follow the example Jesus set forth, then you need to experience this before you proceed operating under your own power.

After His resurrection, Jesus told His disciples to wait until the Holy Spirit had come upon them, with power, to begin their ministries. The Holy Spirit is God, a part of the Holy Trinity. Jesus already knew the importance of having the companionship of the Holy Spirit which helps us understand God's Word, and gives us the power to heal the sick, cast out demons, and to raise the dead. With the Baptism of the Holy Spirit, you will have more confidence and boldness, realizing strength that you alone do not possess.

The good news is that anyone who asks for the Baptism of the Holy Spirit will receive it. Do not let fear, or lack of understanding, prevent you from asking Jesus to baptize you in the Holy Spirit. He said that everyone who asks will receive. Do not be afraid of receiving something other than the Holy Spirit when you ask; God loves you and He will give you that which you desire.

Unquestionably, the Bible mentions the indwelling of the Holy Spirit and tongues many times. Jesus clearly stated that signs and miracles will follow those who believe:

Mark 16:17

"And these signs shall follow those who believe: In My name they will cast out demons; they will speak with new tongues."

Speaking in tongues is one of the definitive evidences of the Baptism of the Holy Spirit, and is something that generally happens quickly for those who have requested the Baptism of the Holy Spirit.

After you ask Jesus for the Baptism of the Holy Spirit you likely will be able to speak with your new tongues, or prayer language. The key is, you must do the speaking, letting sounds and syllables come from your own vocal chords, through your mouth, just as you would in speaking normally. The Holy Spirit depends on you to start the process, out loud, verbally. Simply begin to thank Jesus and praise Him for His many blessings and utter sounds and syllables and then yield to the Holy Spirit to take it from there. It is helpful if you can work with someone who has been through this process, as it will help you get beyond your initial apprehensions regarding this. Remember, everyone's prayer language is different, and yours might start out with very simple sounds, developing more fully as time goes by. The Holy Spirit is a gentleman; He waits for you to start the process. He will not throw you down and take control of your body forcing these sounds to come out of you.

Often, you will immediately feel as if you are doing this, and it is not coming from your spirit. This is one of the lies Satan uses to discourage you, and it is perfectly normal to doubt yourself, but reject these thoughts and you will be fine. As you continue to pray from your spirit, you will notice the power in your prayer life increasing as this is a direct hotline from your spirit to God. Even if you do not understand what you are saying, trust in the fact that the Holy Spirit is communicating your every need, and praise to God. If you find yourself facing a difficult situation and you lack the words to pray effectively, use your prayer language to get the breakthrough you need. Remember, it is there for you to turn it on or off whenever you need it.

Why this phenomenon is such a controversy amongst so many denominations is clearly a mystery as the Bible encourages us to use prayer language, or tongues. It is one of the signs that follow us as believers, and it is for our use in this present day and age. All of the New Testament was written by men who regularly practiced speaking in tongues. Misunderstanding this subject is not reason enough to totally dismiss this concept and eliminate it from doctrine. It will help you understand the Bible more, and give you that added boost of confidence knowing that you are equipped with everything Jesus had to be a more effective minister for Him.

Speaking in your prayer language is not what heals people. It is the power of the Holy Spirit that heals, and that is what this chapter is really all about. With this power, you can move the mountains of sickness and disease, and set the captives free.

Romans 15:13

"Now may the God of hope fill you with all joy and peace in believing, that you may abound in hope by the power of the Holy Spirit."

Initially, as a one-time event, the Apostles of Christ waited until the Holy Spirit fell on them as Jesus had instructed:

Luke 24:49

"Behold, I send the Promise of My Father upon you; but tarry in the city of Jerusalem until you are endued with power from on high."

Acts 2:1-4

"When the day of Pentecost had fully come, they were all with one accord in one place. And suddenly, there came a sound from Heaven, as of a rushing mighty wind, and it filled the whole house where they were sitting. Then there appeared to them divided tongues, as of fire, and one sat upon each of them. And they were all filled with the Holy

Spirit and began to speak with other tongues, as the Spirit gave them utterance."

Thankfully, we no longer have to sit around waiting for the Holy Spirit to fall on us. We simply need to request, from Jesus, the Baptism of the Holy Spirit.

Everyone who has a personal relationship with Jesus Christ can have the Baptism of the Holy Spirit as well. Salvation and the indwelling of the Holy Spirit are two separate occurrences. Jesus is the one who will baptize you in the Holy Spirit if you ask Him. No one is refused. Simply ask, believing He will do what He says.

Luke 11:9-13

"So I say to you, ask, and it will be given to you; seek, and you will find; knock, and it will be opened to you. For everyone who asks receives, and he who seeks finds, and to him who knocks it will be opened. If a son asks for bread from any father among you, will he give him a stone? Or if he asks for a fish, will he give him a serpent instead of a fish? Or if he asks for an egg, will he offer him a scorpion? If you then, being evil, know how to give good gifts to your children, how much more will your heavenly Father give the Holy Spirit to those who ask Him!"

So, now that you see the advantages of being empowered by the Holy Spirit, are you ready to take this important step? Here is a simple prayer for receiving the Baptism of the Holy Spirit:

"Heavenly Father, I want to receive the Baptism of the Holy Spirit, as You promised to those who believe. I believe.

Jesus, please baptize me in the Holy Spirit right now, so that the power of the Holy Spirit will work in me and through me, enabling me to serve You according to Your will and purpose. Holy Spirit, I welcome you, fill me now. I surrender all to You. Help me make a difference for the Kingdom of Heaven and enable me with Your power. In Jesus' name I ask this. Amen!"

God's Word is truth. If you sincerely prayed this prayer, Jesus has immediately answered it.

The fruits of the Holy Spirit include love, joy, peace, longsuffering, kindness, goodness, faithfulness, gentleness and self-control. The Baptism of the Holy Spirit gives you access to these fruits which all reside in your spirit, and can be manifest into your body and soul.

In reality, there is only one gift, and that is the gift of the Holy Spirit. He provides the word of wisdom, the word of knowledge, faith, healing, miracles, prophecy, discernment, tongues, and interpretation of tongues. All of these are diversities, or characteristics made available from the Holy Spirit. These will often manifest for a specific event which is useful in building up the body of Christ in a given situation, such as in a church service. All believers have access to each of these gifts as the Holy Spirit sees fit. It is incorrect to label people as having a particular gift, or anointing. There is not a special anointing needed to heal the sick. It is incorrect to say that a Spiritual First Responder has the gift of healing. You may have this gift bestowed on you for a specific purpose, otherwise you are simply operating in the authority that Jesus gave all believers to heal the sick. We are all of the same Spirit, and

He chooses who operates in these gifts, and for what purpose they serve.

1 Corinthians 12:4-11

"There are diversities of gifts, but the same Spirit. There are differences of ministries, but the same Lord. And there are diversities of activities, but it is the same God who works all in all. But the manifestation of the Spirit is given to each one for the profit of all: for to one is given the word of wisdom through the Spirit, to another the word of knowledge through the same Spirit, to another faith by the same Spirit, to another gifts of healings by the same Spirit, to another the working of miracles, to another prophecy, to another discerning of spirits, to another different kinds of tongues, to another the interpretation of tongues. But one and the same Spirit works all these things, distributing to each one individually as He wills."

Notice that these gifts of the Holy Spirit include and mention tongues. There are two types of tongues mentioned in the Bible. When the Bible speaks of the "gift of tongues", it is very important to remember that this is communication from God, down from Heaven through man, to be interpreted by someone who has been given the gift of interpretation. Our personal prayer language, also known as tongues, represents communication from our spirits to God, as they are a spiritual hotline to Him which allows the Holy Spirit to speak from your spirit directly to God, even when you don't know what to pray for. Pray in your spiritual language often. You will begin to see amazing things happen and experience supernatural, often unexplainable coincidences that will manifest, according to God's will.

Romans 8:26

"Likewise the Spirit also helps in our weaknesses. For we do not know what we should pray for as we ought, but the Spirit Himself makes intercession for us with groanings which cannot be uttered."

Have you ever faced a situation where you simply did not have the wisdom for how you should pray? If so, the Baptism of the Holy Spirit will help you pray effectively.

Ephesians 6:18-20

"Praying always with all prayer and supplication in the Spirit, being watchful to this end with all perseverance and supplication for all the saints - and for me, that utterance may be given to me, that I may open my mouth boldly to make known the mystery of the gospel, for which I am an ambassador in chains; that in it I may speak boldly, as I ought to speak."

Many people try to achieve an emotional experience with the Holy Spirit in their worship services. This becomes the whole objective of their church life. While this seems important, it should not be the primary focus of your Christian life. In other words, get beyond the four walls of your church building and use the power of the Holy Spirit to minister to others. It is not necessary to have the Holy Spirit rain down on a church service; He is already with you. He will never leave you, nor forsake you. Once you invite Him into your life, you have Him for life.

The Holy Spirit can and will manifest in various ways in your life. Let Him alone decide when and where these supernatural manifestations take place. Many churches are starting to concentrate on calling in the Holy Spirit in an effort to seek some sort of visual sign that He is present. These signs may include glory clouds, gold dust, jewels falling from the ceiling, and others. The Holy Spirit may choose to manifest in this way, but that is not His role. These practices are not scriptural, even though they seem harmless. Stick with what the Word says! Let Him endue you with power; let Him be the Helper to you that He is. You do not need a sign, be aware of His presence; honor Him at all times. Be led by the Word of God and let the Holy Spirit help you accomplish His true purpose.

In summary, do not let fear rob you of receiving the power of the Holy Spirit. If you haven't done so, ask Jesus for this gift immediately and then walk in the full power of your relationship with the Holy Spirit.

Here are some scriptures that will help you understand this more clearly:

Romans 8:11

"But if the Spirit of Him who raised Jesus from the dead dwells in you, He who raised Christ from the dead will also give life to your mortal bodies through His Spirit who dwells in you."

1 Corinthians 14:39-40

"Therefore brethren, desire earnestly to prophesy, and do not forbid to speak with tongues. Let all things be done decently and in order."

1 John 5:6-7

"This is He who came by water and blood – Jesus Christ; not only by water, but by water and blood. And it is the Spirit who bears witness, because the Spirit is truth. For there are three that bear witness in Heaven: the Father, the Word, and the Holy Spirit; and these three are one."

Acts 19:6

"And when Paul had laid hands on them, the Holy Spirit came upon them, and they spoke with tongues and prophesied."

1 Corinthians 14:4

"He who speaks in a tongue edifies himself."

Include your favorite scriptures here:

Chapter 5

Your Spiritual Identity

Once you have committed your life to Jesus, and have entered into a personal relationship with Him as your Lord and Savior, it is prudent to learn exactly who you are in Christ. This is known as your Spiritual Identity.

As humans, we are made up of three separate things: body, soul, and spirit. Obviously, your body is your Earth suit which houses your soul and spirit. It is what physically gets us from point to point, and acts out the desires of the soul. It is the physical bridge between our soul and spirit and the world we live in.

Your soul, sometimes referred to as your flesh, is composed of your emotions, thoughts, and feelings. Your soul reports what your body is feeling. It lets you know when you are happy, sad, hungry, tired, angry, scared, or confident. This is known as responding to the flesh. The soul constantly monitors input from our body, and spirit simultaneously. While the body feeds the soul information on its physical condition, the spirit feeds the soul spiritual information. It tells the soul what is right, and what is wrong, what is true, and what is false. The soul is said to be the interface between the spirit and body.

The spirit is sometimes falsely confused with the soul, but it is an entirely different element as stated in scripture. We are spirit beings, and our spirit defines who we are. Our spirits live forever. So, in effect, we are really a spirit being, made in the image of God, which has a soul, and resides in a body.

Immediately upon accepting Christ as your Redeemer, your spirit is renewed, and is perfected. In essence, as the Bible states, you now have the mind of Christ. The Bible refers to this as putting on the New Man. It is up to us to draw on this spiritual reservoir within us to bring the promises of God into our lives through our souls and bodies, by way of our spirit. Your spirit is perfect, but your soul and body are not. The renewing of your mind, or soul, will bring your body into perfect alignment with God's will for your life.

Here, the Bible addresses the soul, spirit, and body as separate entities contained in us as a human being:

Hebrews 4:12

"For the Word of God is living and powerful, and sharper than any two-edged sword, piercing even to the division of soul and spirit, and of joints and marrow, and is a discerner of the thoughts and intents of the heart."

1 Thessalonians 5:23

"Now may the God of peace Himself sanctify you completely; and may your whole spirit, soul, and body be preserved blameless at the coming of our Lord Jesus Christ."

Accepting Christ as Lord and Savior instantly transforms our spirit, causing it to be born again. According to the Bible, every good and perfect gift is given to us. The moment we accept Christ, our spirits become brand new. In effect, we have a new identity, casting aside our former sin nature. We are a completely new person, we are born of God, and we are made alive with God:

2 Corinthians 5:17

"Therefore, if anyone is in Christ, he is a new creation; old things have passed away; behold all things have become new."

This is speaking of our spirits, which are instantly made new the moment we accept Christ. The Bible even tells us that the old man in us has died with Christ, and that we are raised to new life through Christ's resurrection:

Romans 6:4

"Therefore we were buried with Him through baptism into death, that just as Christ was raised from the dead by the glory of the Father, even so we also should walk in newness of life."

A clear distinction must be made here. Our spirits are born again, but our souls are not. The soul must go through a process of cleansing, and this is done by the Word of God through our spirit. This is known as renewing the mind.

Romans 12:2

"And do not be conformed to this world, but be transformed by the renewing of your mind, that you may prove what is that good and acceptable and perfect will of God."

1 Peter 1:22-23

"Since you have purified your souls in obeying the truth through the Spirit in sincere love of the brethren, love one another fervently with a pure heart, having been born again, not of corruptible seed but incorruptible, through the Word of God which lives and abides forever."

We are to put off the old man, and put on the new man through the renewing of our minds.

Ephesians 4:21-24

"If indeed you have heard Him and have been taught by Him, as the truth is in Jesus: that you put off, concerning your former conduct, the old man which grows corrupt according to the deceitful lusts, and be renewed in the spirit of your mind, and that you put on the new man which was created according to God, in true righteousness and holiness."

Satan is powerless to attack your perfected spirit. Your body and soul can be vulnerable to his abilities, however. Renewing your mind closes those open doors that he uses to cause you distress and physical sickness. He has ability, but he does not have the authority to attack you. Unless we close these doors to him, he will seek to exploit every avenue to rob you of your joy, and destroy your life. That is his mission here on Earth, to ruin your life. Concentrate on your identity in Jesus, and eventually, the soul will align itself with the spirit. The soul is capable of manifesting the truth of Jesus, which is in the spirit, outwardly to the body.

The Bible says that every good and perfect gift has already been given to you. Now having all of this in our spirit, it has been downloaded into us the instant we trusted Jesus as Lord and Savior. This means that we do not have to beg God for any good thing, as He has already given us every good thing! It is up to us to draw it out of our spirit,

James 1:17

"Every good gift and every perfect gift is from above, and comes down from the Father of lights, with whom there is no variation or shadow of turning."

The Bible also says that we now have the mind of Christ, and it is perfect. We are now literally Sons of God, joint-heirs with Jesus Christ. The soul, being purified by the Word delivered through the spirit, becomes renewed. Once the mind has been renewed, this gives the soul the ability to manage the body in a Godly way, defeating illness, and taking advantage of other things offered to us as citizens of the Kingdom of God.

When we accept Jesus as Lord and Savior, eternal life begins immediately. It is not something we have to wait on when we die and go to Heaven. It is available to us here and now on planet Earth.

Being born again has its benefits!

In the Kingdom of God, there is no sickness, sorrow, poverty or grief. As citizens of the Kingdom of God, here on Earth, we should expect to experience the same benefits.

The Lord's Prayer says it best:

Matthew 6:8-14

"Therefore do not be like them. For your Father knows the things you have need of before you ask Him. In this manner, therefore, pray:

"Our Father in heaven, hallowed be Your name. Your kingdom come, Your will be done on earth as it is in heaven. Give us this day our daily bread. And forgive us our debts, as we forgive our debtors. And do not lead us into temptation, but deliver us from the evil one. For Yours is the kingdom and the power and the glory forever. Amen."

The Kingdom of God is for the here and now, and not just for when we die. We can experience the happiness, joy, power, and the very will of God today. Your Kingdom come, Your will be done, on Earth as it is in Heaven.

In fact, when we accept Jesus, we have literally been adopted into the family of God.

Romans 8:15

"For you did not receive the spirit of bondage again to fear, but you received the Spirit of adoption by whom we cry out, 'Abba, Father.'"

Galatians 4:6

"And because you are sons, God has sent forth the Spirit of His Son into your hearts, crying out, 'Abba, Father!'"

God gives us permission to call Him Father. If He is our Father, then we are His children. If we are His children, we are heirs to our Father's estate, or Kingdom. Jesus, being the first born, is the true heir, but we are joint heirs with Him, having access to the same benefits of the Kingdom of God. We are granted permission to enter His presence just as if we were His children, because we are.

Romans 8:16-17

"The Spirit Himself bears witness with our spirit that we are children of God, and if children, then heirs - heirs of God and joint heirs with Christ, if indeed we suffer with Him, that we may also be glorified together."

The legal definition of a joint heir is:

A person who shares with another, or others, the right to inherit a person's money, property, or title when that person dies.

There is incredible power and there are vast resources available to those who are in Christ having a perfected spirit. Literally, you instantly become a joint-heir to the Kingdom of God, complete with all of the benefits that come with it. The Bible says we are instantly transformed and become Sons of God, just like Jesus. When we are able to renew our minds, or souls, to think as the spirit thinks, we can see physical manifestations of the Kingdom here in our present lives. Such is the excitement of seeing miracles happen before your very eyes, just as in the days of Jesus. Since He now dwells in you, it is your obligation to be an ambassador of the Kingdom of God letting Him heal through your obedience. You are now His voice, His hands, His transportation from place to place. You carry the Spirit of Jesus in your spirit.

Renewing of the mind is crucial if you expect to be an effective Spiritual First Responder. This is simply training the soul and body to operate out of the desires of your perfected spirit, instead of the emotions of your soul. Taking every thought captive and comparing it to what the

Word of God says is a good way to start the process of renewing your mind. For example, if you receive a bad medical report, you can now believe it when the Bible says that Jesus paid the price for your healing. If someone tells you that it is impossible to do a task, your spirit now tells you that all things are possible through Christ.

Speaking from the spirit will cause you to speak the truth. Speaking from your flesh will cause you to speak doubt, and fear at times. The Bible says that the power of life and death are in the words that we speak. Therefore, it is best to speak from your spirit claiming life, more abundantly. When your soul hears your spirit proclaim the truth, it begins to believe and accept it as the truth. Doing this will cause physical manifestations to occur in your own body, as well. You can learn to walk in Divine health with a renewed mind. You can enjoy the provisions of God and His prosperity in your life using these same techniques when it comes to relationships, finances and other areas in your life.

It is important to understand your identity in Christ. Knowing who you are, and that you are an Ambassador of the Kingdom of God is what gives you the ultimate authority to practice as a Spiritual First Responder. You are worthy, and you were worthy the minute you accepted the gift of God's grace through your faith and belief in Jesus.

You do not have to be totally sanctified and holy to heal the sick. Do not wait until you feel like your soul is perfected and renewed to get started. Obeying the command of Jesus to heal the sick is part of this renewal process. Do not put ministry off waiting for a feeling from your flesh. Do as your spirit encourages you to do, and go heal the sick.

You are born again. You are a new creation. You are renewing your mind daily, putting on the New Man. You are a joint heir to the Kingdom of God. You are a son of God. Understanding your identity in Jesus is crucial.

Your power lies in the fact that Jesus dwells within you. Remember, our weapons are spiritual, not carnal and of the flesh. If you are to destroy the works of the enemy, you must do so with a renewed mind.

In summary, cast off the Old Man, and renew your mind and body to the perfect truth of the Word of God. We are now joint-heirs with Christ to the Kingdom of God, literally as Sons of God.

Here are some scriptures for further reference:

Romans 12:2

"And do not be conformed to this world, but be transformed by the renewing of your mind, that you may prove what is that good and acceptable and perfect will of God."

2 Corinthians 4:16

"Therefore we do not lose heart. Even though our outward man is perishing, yet the inward man is being renewed day by day."

2 Corinthians 5:17

"Therefore, if anyone is in Christ, he is a new creation; old things have passed away; behold all things have become new."

Ephesians 4:21-24

"If indeed you have heard Him and have been taught by Him, as the truth is in Jesus: that you put off, concerning your former conduct, the old man which grows corrupt according to the deceitful lusts, and be renewed in the spirit of your mind, and that you put on the new man which was created according to God, in true righteousness and holiness."

John 1:12-13

"But as many received Him, to them He gave the right to become children of God, to those who believe in His name: who were born, not of blood, nor of the will of the flesh, nor of the will of man, but of God."

1 Thessalonians 5:23

"Now may the God of peace Himself sanctify you completely; and may your whole spirit, soul, and body be preserved blameless at the coming of our Lord Jesus Christ."

Include your favorite scriptures here:

Chapter 6

The Believer's Authority

A policeman has the authority to enforce the laws of the community he is sworn to protect. He is backed by the laws of that community, and can act as a representative to enforce such codes of conduct. He wears a badge, and carries the firepower necessary to bring any situation under control, according to predefined parameters in which he is allowed to operate.

Likewise you, as a Spiritual First Responder, are authorized by the Word of God to destroy the works of the enemy, Satan. You have full authority and are backed by the entire resources of the Kingdom of God. You may, or may not carry a badge, but you have all the tools necessary to bring spiritual situations under control.

There is a spiritual battle going on for the hearts and minds of humanity. On one hand, God is offering salvation through His son Jesus. On the other hand, Satan is attempting to destroy the mind and body, causing everlasting separation between man and God.

Just because you are unaware of this battle, doesn't mean it is not taking place. It simply means you are going to lose the battle. The Bible says my people perish from lack of knowledge. Ignoring this battle does not make it go away. We as Christians must exercise our Believer's Authority to win.

Jesus came to Earth to destroy the works of the devil, and restore man's relationship with God. He returned dominion over the Earth to man, which had been lost when Adam and Eve surrendered it to Satan. The Bible says all authority has been given to Jesus, leaving the devil no authority.

Matthew 28:18-19

"And Jesus spoke to them, saying, 'All authority has been given to me in Heaven and on Earth. Go therefore and make disciples of all nations, baptizing them in the name of the Father and of the Son and of the Holy Spirit.'"

The Great Commission of Jesus Christ orders us to go and make disciples of all nations, by use of the authority of His name. He has all authority, leaving the devil none, and you none. However, you can use the authority of His name.

Luke 10:19-20

"Behold, I give you authority to trample on serpents and scorpions, and over all the power of the enemy, and nothing by any means shall hurt you. Nevertheless do not rejoice in this, that the spirits are subject to you, but rather rejoice because your names are written in Heaven."

Jesus said that all authority in Heaven and Earth has been given to Him. If He has it all, then Satan has none. The devil has ability to cause problems, but he possesses no authority to do so. For example, a robber has the ability to break into a house, but he certainly has no authority to do so. Satan will try to get away with anything he can to slow you down spiritually, even if it means making you sick, or worse, killing you. He is out to kill, steal and destroy, walking to and fro like a roaring lion seeking to devour us. Yes, he is getting away with it because of a lack of

Christians using their God given authority to stop him in his tracks. So, in reality, we are commanded to stop Satan!

Here is where the Believer's Authority comes in to fend off the enemy. Before He left to go back to Heaven, Jesus commanded us to use the authority of His name to destroy the works of the enemy. The Bible says that every knee will bow to the name of Jesus, and all power is available to us through the use of that name. We are given permission to trample on the scorpions of sin, including casting out demons, healing the sick, and even raising the dead.

We are told to resist the devil.

James 4:7

"Therefore submit to God. Resist the devil and he will flee from you."

You need every weapon available to you in conducting spiritual warfare.

2 Corinthians 10:4

"For the weapons of our warfare are not carnal but mighty in God for pulling down strongholds,"

We need the full armor of God to battle the devil.

Ephesians 6:11-13

"Put on the whole armor of God, that you may be able to stand against the wiles of the devil. For we do not wrestle against flesh and blood, but against principalities, against powers, against the rulers of the darkness of this age, against spiritual hosts of wickedness in the heavenly places. Therefore take up the whole armor of God, that you may be able to withstand in the evil day, and having done all, to stand."

Here is a list of the pieces of our armor:

Ephesians 6:14-20

"Stand therefore, having girded your waist with truth, having put on the breastplate of righteousness, and having shod your feet with the preparation of the gospel of peace; above all, taking the shield of faith with which you will be able to quench all the fiery darts of the wicked one. And take the helmet of salvation, and the sword of the Spirit, which is the word of God; praying always with all prayer and supplication in the Spirit, being watchful to this end with all perseverance and supplication for all the saints - and for me, that utterance may be given to me, that I may open my mouth boldly to make known the mystery of the gospel, for which I am an ambassador in chains; that in it I may speak boldly, as I ought to speak."

We are taught how to use the Believer's Authority through the healings administered by Jesus, and His apostles, as depicted in the gospels.

Knowing you have access to this authority is crucial to your success as a Spiritual First Responder. When you are sure of your spiritual identity, and your legal right to use the name of Jesus and its authority, you have what it takes to heal the sick, cast out demons, and raise the dead. Be bold in your use of this authority.

Philippians 2:9-10

"Therefore God also has highly exalted Him and given Him the name which is above every name, that at the name of Jesus every knee shall bow, of those in Heaven, and those on Earth, and of those under the Earth."

Romans 8:38-39

"For I am persuaded that neither death nor life, nor angels nor principalities nor powers, nor things present nor things to come, nor height nor depth, nor any other created thing, shall be able to separate us from the love of God which is in Christ Jesus our Lord."

We now, through Jesus, actually have more authority than Adam and Eve had. Adam had authority over the Earth, and we have authority over everything on the Earth, and below the Earth, meaning power over evil spirits.

Satan is the author of destruction. He is capable of attacking you with sickness, mental torment, and more. With the authority granted to us through the name of Jesus, we can overcome these by binding the demonic forces that seek to harm us. Remember, since Jesus has been given all authority, then Satan has zero authority! We are authorized by Jesus to use His authority.

With this authority comes the responsibility to use it. If we fail to use the Believer's Authority, we limit God's ability to intervene in the situation. The warfare is left up to us, but the battle is the Lord's. We have to do our part by exercising the authority over the devil, and He will do His part in enforcing your actions through His power. He has given us the authority to use His power, but He executes it when we exercise the authority. If we do not resist the devil, he will not flee. God will not come and cause the devil to leave on our behalf. It is up to us to force him to flee.

God gave us the power to heal. It is under our authority through the name of Jesus. He never told us to pray for the sick, or to beg God to heal people. He has given us the power to heal the sick through the Believer's Authority.

Here is a perfect example of Peter and John's use of the Believer's Authority:

Acts 3:1-8

"Now Peter and John went up together to the temple at the hour of prayer, the ninth hour. And a certain man lame from his mother's womb was carried, whom they laid daily at the gate of the temple which is called Beautiful, to ask alms from those who entered the temple; who, seeing Peter and John about to go into the temple, asked for alms. And fixing his eyes on him, with John, Peter said, 'Look at us.' So he gave them his attention, expecting to receive something from them. Then Peter said, 'Silver and gold I do not have, but what I do have I give you: In the name of Jesus Christ of Nazareth, rise up and walk.' And he took him by the right hand and lifted him up, and immediately his feet and ankle bones received strength. So he, leaping up, stood and walked and entered the temple with them—walking, leaping, and praising God."

Peter said he had the authority to heal. He healed this lame man, and he did not pray to God to get it done. In fact, he was on the way to the temple to pray. This puts to rest the notion that you have to be super spiritual, or in perfect harmony with God to make healing work. It is not God's responsibility to heal; it is ours through the use of the name of Jesus. Again, it's our responsibility to make it happen.

You heal the sick out of your spirit, not out of your emotions. You do not have to petition God to make healing happen, as He has already paid the price for all healing. It is now up to you to get the job done.

Mark 16:17-18

"And these things will follow those who believe: In My name they will cast out demons, they will speak with new tongues, they will take up serpents; and if they drink anything deadly, it will by no means hurt them; they will lay hands on the sick, and they will recover."

If you believe that the Bible is the infallible, inspired Word of God, embrace Jesus as your Lord and Savior, operate in the power of the Holy Spirit, and understand the Believer's Authority, then you have all the firepower you need to bring spiritual situations under control. You are prepared for spiritual warfare, with the confidence of knowing your enemy is already defeated. This is a great tactical position to be in, but you must believe it with all your heart. The weapons we use are spiritual, and not carnal, meaning we fight with our spirits. We let our bodies and minds stand down while our spirit directs the fight, all the while the Jesus within us is fighting the fight for us. The battle is not ours, it is the Lord's. We fight with love, with truth, and we win, every time.

This power was given to you as part of your inheritance in Jesus Christ. You have entered into this position of authority because of Him. The benefits of being a child of God are incredible. Be ready in season and out of season to exercise this authority.

In summary, you as a Spiritual First Responder have every tool at your disposal to bring about a positive resolution to any spiritual matter through the use of the Believer's Authority.

Here are some scriptures that describe this in more detail:

Luke 10:19-20

"Behold, I give you authority to trample on serpents and scorpions, and over all the power of the enemy, and nothing by any means shall hurt you. Nevertheless do not rejoice in this, that the spirits are subject to you, but rather rejoice because your names are written in Heaven."

Philippians 2:9-10

"Therefore God also has highly exalted Him and given Him the name which is above every name, that at the name of Jesus every knee shall bow, of those in Heaven, and those on Earth, and of those under the Earth."

Matthew 28:18-19

"And Jesus spoke to them, saying, 'All authority has been given to me in Heaven and on Earth. Go therefore and make disciples of all nations, baptizing them in the name of the Father and of the Son and of the Holy Spirit.'"

James 4:7

"Therefore submit to God. Resist the devil and he will flee from you."

Romans 8:31

"What then shall we say to these things? If God is for us, who can be against us?"

1 John 4:4

"You are of God little children, and have overcome them, because He who is in you is greater than he that is in the world."

Colossians 1:12-13

"He has delivered us from the power of darkness and conveyed us into the kingdom of the Son of His Love, in whom we have redemption through His blood, the forgiveness of sins."

Include your favorite scriptures here:

Chapter 7

Traditions of Men

There are only a couple of things that can affect your mission as a Spiritual First Responder. One is a lack of faith or belief, which we will discuss briefly, and the other is known as "traditions of men".

You can strengthen your faith by immersing yourself in the Word of God. Read about the ministry of Jesus, observing any and all verses that deal with faith and belief. The Bible says that faith comes by hearing, and hearing by the Word of God. Associate yourself, if possible, with other trained Spiritual First Responders that are walking in power. The more you see successful miracles taking place, the stronger your faith will be. Your unconditional belief, along with even the smallest measure of faith, are the ingredients that will propel your ministry to success.

Traditions of men are beliefs that are widely held, and often taught in major denominations, that if believed, can weaken your ability to see miracles happen. If you have been brought up in one of these denominations, you will recognize some of the traditions of men listed in this section. This is by no means an exhaustive study of these beliefs, but an effort to show how they work against your mission as a Spiritual First Responder.

Mark 7:13

"Making the Word of God of no effect through your tradition which you have handed down. And many such things you do."

Since we know the Bible is the true Word of God, we understand what it means when it says the traditions of men make the Word of God ineffective. These beliefs attack your common sense, faith, and authority by challenging your spiritual identity. Frankly, it is easier to believe that miracles no longer happen, until you need one. It takes no faith to believe that the miracles of Christ and His apostles were meant for that time period alone.

Those that believe that miracles ceased to exist after the writing of the Bible are known as cessationists. It is their assumption that the miracles displayed during the ministry of Jesus were performed to establish the Divinity of Jesus. It worked then, and it still works now. Jesus commanded His disciples to heal the sick, cleanse the lepers, cast out demons, and to raise the dead. He has never rescinded that command. He ordered them to go make new disciples teaching them to do all things, just like He did. You, as a Spiritual First Responder are a disciple of Christ. The first time you see a miracle happen in front of you, this cessationists' argument will be a moot point. You will know that God still heals today. There may even be those that attribute your success to the devil, but you are in good company, as the religious leaders of the day said the exact same thing about Jesus. We know better. You will encounter many such arguments, just keep pressing on.

It is worth mentioning here that as a Spiritual First Responder, your mission is not to get into deep theological discussions with others, as doing so only delays you from getting your stated mission accomplished. The absolute best way to end any argument about this is to heal someone in front of a non-believer. Even then, it is amazing how many will deny what just happened before their very eyes. If possible, when practicing healing, don't let people speak out in unbelief. If they are not part of the solution, they very well may be part of the problem. There will be time to direct healed and sick people to a Bible believing church once you have ministered to them. You are there to stabilize the situation, and then introduce them to further knowledge. Getting into any arguments before you minister is counter-productive. You likely will encounter many people using traditions of men as an excuse to justify their illness, or lack of being healed. Do not allow these arguments to interfere with your attempts to minister to such people. Get the job done, and then teach them what the Bible really says about healing. Do not allow their unbelief to hinder your efforts.

Here is another way to look at this:

A paramedic's job is to come on the scene, and medically stabilize the situation. After doing so, the patient is transported to the hospital for full care and restoration back to health. It is not the job of the paramedic to argue with a doctor over the two-way radio about treatment. He gets his job done by performing the duties he is trained to do. Then it is up to the hospital to see the patient through his recovery. Likewise, you as a Spiritual First Responder have to stabilize the situation with ministry, and then direct the person to a Bible believing church for further restoration.

There are literally thousands of people in need of healing. Keep moving, and don't let the ones who want to argue with you slow you down. Leave the scene, then pray.

Some people actually believe that God puts sickness on them to punish them for their sins, or to teach them a lesson through their suffering. Obviously unfamiliar with the concept of grace, these misinformed people will wind up going to a doctor, oddly enough, to become well, thereby subverting the perceived will of God in their lives. They will sometimes reference Job, claiming God allowed the devil to attack him. The book of Job clearly states that the devil took it upon himself to attack Job, evoking the wrath of God. Under the Old Covenant, this story has a happy ending with God fully restoring Job double his original losses. Jesus never once put a sickness on anyone to teach them a lesson. The Bible says He healed them all.

Job 42:10

"And the Lord restored Job's losses when he prayed for his friends. Indeed the Lord gave Job twice as much as he had before."

What about Paul's thorn? It was said to be an ailment that affected the Apostle Paul's eyesight. If healing works today, why wasn't Paul healed of this condition back during the days of the early church?

2 Corinthians 12:7

"And lest I should be exalted above measure by the abundance of the revelations, a thorn in the flesh was given to me, a messenger of Satan to buffet me, lest I be exalted above measure."

Here, the apostle Paul clearly tells us it was a messenger from Satan, and not any type of disease or illness. Any time the word thorn is used in the Bible, it references a person, never an illness. Out of all the suffering Paul went through for the Gospel, he never mentions sickness. Paul referred to his suffering as infirmities. He mentions beatings, hunger, thirst, shipwrecks, being stoned, and more. However, he never mentions being sick at all. Even Jesus made it clear that there is a difference between an infirmity or weakness, and a sickness:

Mathew 8:16-17

"When evening had come, they brought to Him many who were demon-possessed. And He cast out the spirits with a word, and healed all who were sick, that it might be fulfilled which was spoken by Isaiah the prophet, saying:

'He Himself took our infirmities and bore our sicknesses.'"

It is often said that Jesus could not heal anyone in His hometown. Here is the scripture reference used when people make this argument:

Mark 6:5

"Now He could do no mighty work there, except that He laid His hands on a few sick people and healed them."

In the hometown of Jesus, people recognized Him as the son of Joseph and Mary, not realizing He was actually the Son of God. They knew him as a son of a carpenter, not a worker of miracles. Likely, they did not throng to Him as people did in other cities where He ministered. It stands to reason, that if not many came to Jesus for a miracle, then fewer miracles would be performed. Still, even though the Bible says that He could do no great miracles, it clearly says that He did, in fact, heal people. This is perfectly obvious in scripture, refuting this often taught doctrine.

Here, we see how scripture has been misquoted, or truncated to avoid the truth. People who rely on traditions of men are simply looking for excuses for being powerless.

It is not God's will that everyone should be healed.

This comes from the Doctrine of Sovereignty which teaches that God is responsible for everything that happens, good or bad. This is a very dangerous teaching, as it causes total apathy in the Christian life. This is an easy teaching to fall prey to, as it shifts our personal responsibility over to God. It is much easier to believe that God is in control of everything, but this is simply not true. He is not keeping a giant scorecard on every person determining who gets healed, or not. Jesus told us to heal the sick. He never said that God would pick and choose who gets healed, and who doesn't. In scripture, it states that Jesus healed them all. Over and over this is repeated. Never once did He tell someone that they didn't measure up to His standards, or that they needed to wait awhile to work some better good in their life. No, Jesus healed them all. When a leper approached Jesus, He told him that it was His will to heal him:

Mark 1:40-41

"Now a leper came to Him, imploring Him, kneeling down to Him and saying to Him, 'If You are willing, You can make me clean.' Then Jesus, moved with compassion, stretched out His hand and touched him, and said to him, 'I am willing; be cleansed.'"

Jesus displayed the will of the Father, because He was God in the flesh.

John 14:7

"If you had known Me, you would have known My Father also; and from now on you know Him and have seen Him."

There are at least seventeen passages in the New Testament that indicate that Jesus healed everyone He came into contact with that needed it. Again, nowhere does it say that Jesus intentionally left someone sick, or reluctantly healed someone. It is always the will of the Father to heal. Jesus said He had come to give life more abundantly:

John 10:10

"The thief does not come except to steal, and to kill, and to destroy. I have come that they may have life, and that they may have it more abundantly."

Some people believe that it takes great faith to heal, or be healed. Signs and wonders follow those who believe. The miracles you will see are great ministry opportunities. You will actually see atheists healed in the name of Jesus. The typical atheist has no faith whatsoever in Jesus, yet they can be healed instantly. Also, brand new converts who accept Jesus have immediate power to heal the sick. Yes, immediate power, as you will see in the course of your ministry. Simple child-like faith can bring about miracles. Jesus is awesome, and since He has already paid the price for healing, it makes our obedience to Him more productive.

Throughout your journey as a Spiritual First Responder, you will encounter many traditions of men. Learn to recognize them, and ignore them. In all cases, remember that the Word of God authorizes you to heal the sick. You must believe this, and know that any argument that tries to disrupt your belief is not of God. There is no room for apology here, this is the truth.

In summary, evaluate everything you have been taught about miracles. Go to the Word of God for your information and know that these miracles still take place, quite often, in this present day and age.

Here are some supporting scriptures that you may find helpful:

Hosea 4:6

"My people are destroyed for lack of knowledge."

Mark 16:17-18

"And these things will follow those who believe: In My name they will cast out demons, they will speak with new tongues, they will take up serpents; and if they drink anything deadly, it will by no means hurt them; they will lay hands on the sick, and they will recover."

Include your favorite scriptures here:

Chapter 8

Healing the Sick

Here is where we begin to put into action the truths we have reviewed in the previous chapters. If you have skipped ahead in an effort to jumpstart your ministry, you are doing yourself and those you work with, a great disservice. Please carefully review all of the information presented previously and make sure you completely understand the material before you continue with your efforts. Information is powerful. The more you understand, the better your success rate will be.

One thing that is of paramount importance is understanding exactly what you are called to do, and knowing what you should avoid doing. Jesus commands us to lay hands on the sick, so they can recover. That is the primary function of the Spiritual First Responder. Many people you will come in contact with are under the care of a doctor and are on medications that help them deal with the illness or pain they are afflicted with. Under no circumstances should you ever suggest that a person discontinue their medications, unless specifically directed to do so by their doctor. Avoid discussing medications altogether if possible, and never, ever offer information about medicine, or other medical treatments. You are not a doctor, and your job is not to practice medicine, but to simply offer spiritual support and encouragement to the sick and hurting. Even if you actually know the best course for medical treatment, avoid the temptation and decline to discuss it. Do your part, and give Jesus the credit for a manifested miracle.

Have you ever wondered why many people die of sickness?

Healing is an accomplished act. It is not something we have to say, or do that makes it happen. In fact, we cannot make God heal anyone, He has already done it. Asking Him to do it again is redundancy. No amount of pleading or begging God will ever move Him to heal a single person. You can get ten thousand people to form a prayer chain, begging God to move in a situation, and it will likely not work. God's will is that everyone be well, and that none should perish. The truth is, He commands us to heal the sick.

There are millions of people who are praying ineffectively for healing. It is obvious that this is true because so many never realize the healing they are praying for. So, what is the problem? Is it God refusing to heal, or is it ineffective prayer? Praying the wrong way has its consequences. There are Kingdom laws that God has put into place that He Himself will not even violate. He has already paid the price for healing; He has commanded us to heal the sick through our Believer's Authority. There are few exceptions. God is no respecter of persons. He is not going to do something He told you to do. It is by grace that we are saved, even healed, through faith, and not of works, lest any man should boast.

Ephesians 2:8-9

"For by grace you have been saved through faith, and not of yourselves; it is the gift of God, not of works, lest anyone should boast."

Faith is the key, not works. You cannot expect to move God to answer your prayers by the things you do. No amount of Bible reading, confession, witnessing, church attendance, or buying power will cause a miracle to manifest. No, it is through faith that these things happen, because God has made this available to you through His grace. He has already given us every perfect gift from above. Your goodness has nothing to do with your ability to get healed, or your ability to minister healing to others.

James 1:17

"Every good gift and every perfect gift is from above, and comes down from the Father of lights, with whom there is no variation or shadow of turning."

Ephesians 1:3

"Blessed be the God and Father of our Lord Jesus Christ, who has blessed us with every spiritual blessing in the heavenly places in Christ."

The truth of the matter is that you already possess everything you need in your spirit to see healing manifest for you and others. You have the same spirit in you that raised Christ from the dead.

Romans 8:11

"But if the Spirit of Him who raised Jesus from the dead dwells in you, He who raised Christ from the dead will also give life to your mortal bodies through His Spirit who dwells in you."

Healing was paid for in the Atonement of Christ. His beating at the whipping post before He was crucified has healed our sicknesses. Many doctrines teach that this healing is for our sins, but Matthew plainly states that He bodily healed all so the prophecy of Isaiah would be fulfilled.

Isaiah 53:4-5

"Surely He has borne our griefs and carried our sorrows; yet we esteemed Him stricken, smitten by God, and afflicted. But He was wounded for our transgressions, He was bruised for our iniquities; the chastisement for our peace was upon Him, and by His stripes we are healed."

Notice it says we "are" healed, meaning it was foretold to happen in the future.

Here is where Matthew confirms the prophecy:

Matthew 8:16-17

"When evening had come, they brought to Him many who were demon possessed. And He cast out the spirits with a word, and healed all who were sick, that it might be fulfilled which was spoken by Isaiah the prophet, saying: 'He Himself took our infirmities and bore our sicknesses.'"

Here, in 1 Peter, this passage about healing is mentioned again:

1 Peter 2:24

"Who Himself bore our sins in His own body on the tree, that we, having died to sins, might live for righteousness – by whose stripes you were healed."

Notice here that it says by whose stripes you "were" healed. This is in the past tense, meaning it has already been accomplished.

Jesus has already paid the price for all healing. The prophet Isaiah discusses this and says we are healed by His stripes. More specifically, when the Bible mentions salvation, the Greek word sozo is used. This word actually refers to redemption of sin, deliverance from evil, and healing of the body. It is a package deal that encompasses all three provisions made in the Atonement of Jesus Christ.

Here is the Greek definition of sozo:

To save, keep safe and sound, to rescue one from danger or destruction (from injury or peril)

To save a suffering one (from perishing), i.e. one suffering from disease, to make well, heal, restore to health

To preserve one who is in danger of destruction, to save or rescue

To save in the technical biblical sense

As a Spiritual First Responder, we are trained to heal, deliver, and save the sick through the power of the Holy Spirit.

God saves, and heals us all. It is available to all who believe in Jesus, accepting what He did at Calvary. This fact is mentioned many times in the Bible, always coupling healing with salvation:

Psalm 103:2-3

"Bless the Lord, oh my soul, and forget not all His benefits: Who forgives all your iniquities, Who heals all your diseases."

The prophecy mentioned in Isaiah was verified by Matthew in the New Testament, and also by Peter. Jesus was beaten for the healing of our bodies. He took upon Himself every disease and sickness that ever was, and ever will be. He only had to do this once, and it is exactly the same concept employed regarding his shed blood for the remission of all sins, past, present and future. People readily accept Christ as their Savior, but many churches neglect to inform them that He can be accepted as their deliverer and healer, as well. The Psalmist said that He forgives all our sins, and heals all our diseases. It is a package deal, it is already complete, and does not need to be done over and over again.

Healing was a big part of Jesus' ministry here on Earth. By His example, His disciples learned healing, His apostles learned, and so did countless other ordinary believers. In the book of Mark, the last eleven recorded words of Jesus emphasize how important this is to Him, saying believers shall lay hands on the sick, and they shall recover. Immediately thereafter, He was caught up and ascended to be seated at the right hand of God the Father. On Earth, it was the last words He uttered. There has never been a time when Jesus rescinded His command for us to heal the sick.

It is so very important to make sure you are armed with this information before you proceed. Take a few moments to reflect on the validity of the Word of God, your personal relationship with Jesus Christ, your identity in Him, the power of the Holy Spirit, and your Believer's Authority. You must absolutely know what you believe before you can realize success in being a Spiritual First Responder. You must completely agree that Jesus has already paid the price in full for our healing, and He expects us to go forth and lay hands on the sick helping them to recovery. If you doubt any of these facts, spend time in the Word of God and ask the Holy Spirit to reveal the truth to you.

It surprises most people to learn that Jesus never once prayed for a sick person in all of recorded scripture. He commanded us to heal the sick, not pray for the sick. He clearly led by example, setting the standard for how we should approach healing the sick.

Through experience, we have learned that there are three basic forms of Divine Healing. These are: Your faith healing your own body, getting your body healed by someone else's faith, and your faith healing someone else's body. These sound similar, but different techniques are used to accomplish each one of them. Faith is the common denominator that seems to be required in each scenario. You can also see healing manifest through a one-time gift of healing as bestowed on you by the Holy Spirit.

You can be healed by your own faith.

Consider the woman with an issue of blood, making her way through the crowd to reach Jesus. She had been dealing with this for over twelve years, yet she knew exactly what she needed to do in order to get healed:

Mark 5:25-29

"Now a certain woman had a flow of blood for twelve years, and had suffered many things from many physicians. She had spent all that she had and was no better, but rather grew worse. When she heard about Jesus, she came behind Him in the crowd and touched His garment. For she said, 'If only I may touch His clothes, I shall be made well.' Immediately the fountain of her blood was dried up, and she felt in her body that she was healed of the affliction."

It is possible for someone else's faith to get you healed. There have been instances of people standing in by proxy and believing for someone else's healing. There are examples of this in the Bible such as the Roman centurion exhibiting enough faith to get his servant back home healed. If you are unable to physically attend a healing service, or cannot get a personal visit, ask someone to go and stand in for you. There is nothing wrong with this tactic as it exhibits your faith as well.

Matthew 8:5-13

"Now when Jesus had entered Capernaum, a centurion came to Him, pleading with Him, saying, 'Lord, my servant is lying at home paralyzed, dreadfully tormented.' And Jesus said to him, 'I will come and heal him.' The centurion answered and said, 'Lord, I am not worthy that You should come under my roof. But only speak a word, and my servant will be healed. For I also am a man under authority, having soldiers under me. And I say to this one, 'Go,' and he goes; and to another, 'Come,' and he comes; and to my servant, 'Do this,' and he does it.' When Jesus heard it, He marveled, and said to those who followed, 'Assuredly, I say to you, I have not found such great faith, not even in Israel! And I say to you that many will come from east and west, and sit down with Abraham, Isaac, and Jacob in the kingdom of heaven. But the sons of the kingdom will be cast out into outer darkness. There will be weeping and gnashing of teeth.' Then Jesus said to the centurion, 'Go your way; and as you have believed, so let it be done for you.' And his servant was healed that same hour."

Newer Christians, who have not yet learned to walk in Divine health, can call upon the elders of the church to have the Prayer of Faith prayed over them. Here, the practice of anointing with oil is mentioned, but is not totally necessary as our anointing comes with administering the power of the Holy Spirit. In a literal sense, this anointing with oil would necessitate what we are commanded to do, initiate contact through personal touch.

James 5:14-15

"Is anyone among you sick? Let him call for the elders of the church, and let them pray over him, anointing him with oil in the name of the Lord. And the prayer of faith will save the sick, and the Lord will raise Him up. And if he has committed sins, he will be forgiven."

Finally, it is possible to heal someone else using your faith. This is usually done through the Believer's Authority, being confident that Jesus has already paid the price for healing. With this authority, you are able to cast off the offending spirits and command the body to be in submission to the healing authority of God, through using the name of Jesus.

Matthew 28:18-19

"And Jesus spoke to them, saying, 'All authority has been given to me in Heaven and on Earth. Go therefore and make disciples of all nations, baptizing them in the name of the Father and of the Son and of the Holy Spirit.'"

Matthew 10:1

"And when He had called His twelve disciples to Him, He gave them power over unclean spirits, to cast them out, and to heal all kinds of sickness and all kinds of disease."

Mark 16:17-18

"And these things will follow those who believe: In My name they will cast out demons, they will speak with new tongues, they will take up serpents; and if they drink anything deadly, it will by no means hurt them; they will lay hands on the sick, and they will recover."

It is a misconception that great faith is always required to accomplish healing. If you are born again, you already possess faith. You have to have faith to believe in the promises Jesus has for you. If you are born again, you already have received healing as it was provided for you in the Atonement. Jesus says you can even move mountains with the faith of a mustard seed. You simply need to believe that healing is yours, and move to destroy the works of the devil that has attacked your body with sickness. You can learn to walk in Divine health, avoiding the need for personal healing since sickness will not attack you. Jesus said "Only believe" when you are ministering healing or deliverance. A tiny bit of faith and real belief are required.

Demonic spirits are real. It is their mission to produce havoc in the lives of believers and non-believers. It is true that a saved person's spirit is protected, but their bodies and souls can be vulnerable to demonic attack. Many churches draw the line here and refuse to believe that a Christian can come under a demonic influence. The first time you command a spirit of affliction to leave a Christian and you see immediate results, this will be a moot point. You will not have to ever again convince yourself that demonic activity can take place in the lives of Christians.

The subject of demons and evil spirits causes great discomfort amongst many denominations. Some people think that all the demons live in Africa, and are completely unaware of their presence in everyday life. Then again, some people do not want to believe they are real, but they are. They are the cause of many diseases, and pain. They can cause blindness, deafness, and a host of other anomalies. The good news is, they are defeated and we are to cast them out in the name of Jesus. Here is where your Believer's Authority comes into play. We are indeed instructed to cast them out, but you really don't need to spend lots of time chatting with them. The devil would like nothing more than to divert your efforts. Do as Jesus did, tell them to go!

Ephesians 6:12

"For we do not wrestle against flesh and blood, but against principalities, against powers, against the rulers of the darkness of this age, against spiritual hosts of wickedness in the heavenly places."

Luke 4:41

"And demons also came out of many, crying out and saying, 'You are the Christ, the Son of God!' And He, rebuking them, did not allow them to speak, for they knew that He was the Christ."

Your goal as a Spiritual First Responder is to evaluate the situation and take appropriate spiritual action. Heed the call to help the sick recover, just like Jesus did. The Bible says that Jesus healed them all. That included thousands and thousands of people with all types of sicknesses. He used healing as a sign of His Divinity. That is exactly what we should do; making healing a top priority as it is a sign that accompanies us as believers and is useful for spreading the Gospel by demonstration of power. Heal the sick, and then tell them about the Kingdom of Heaven.

Jesus plus anything else is more than you need to get the job done. Avoid formulas that trap you with traditions of men. Stay away from teaching that says you must put people through long counseling sessions before they can be healed. This is not found anywhere in the Bible. If you think about it, Jesus could not have possibly had the time to heal the thousands of people He did using these modern day Christian psychology techniques. There are entire doctrines built around Christian Psychology for healing. Stay away from these. They seek to venture into your childhood exploring your relationship with parents and siblings telling you that it relates to your dealings with the Father, Son, and Holy Spirit. This is absolutely unscriptural, and is nothing more than adding to what the Bible says should otherwise be a simple, straightforward, process.

Likewise, avoid teachings that try to pinpoint disease processes associated with various sinful behaviors. They may say that arthritis is caused by lack of forgiveness, or that asthma is rooted in fear and anxiety. The list goes on and on, and these are all conjecture at best. These well-meaning people that teach these doctrines are really looking for an excuse of why they are not walking in power. If they can somehow shift the blame onto the person being healed, they are off the hook for getting the job done.

At best, you are guessing, and Jesus can heal them without you trying to figure out what caused their ailment. You are likely to inhibit your success by trying to over-analyze the situation. It is what it is, let the Jesus in you handle it and move on.

This brings up an interesting point. If you fail to see an immediate manifestation of a healing, never ever blame the person who is to be healed. Most of all, never blame it on Jesus, either. Just because you don't physically see a manifestation, do not ever say it did not work. There are unseen forces operating in the supernatural world. You can rest assured that if you did your part, things are starting to move. Sometimes it takes more than one attempt to get a healing to manifest. Don't be afraid to try it again, after all Jesus did the very same thing when He worked with a blind man twice to restore his sight. Never pull your faith back by saying it did not work. It can happen the minute you walk away or even later that night while the person is asleep. There will be times such as this that test your faith, but don't give in to discouragement, be determined to keep trying. Persistence will pay off. In most cases, the people you minister to are not expecting immediate results anyway. This is why healing can be such a powerful ministry opportunity when immediate results do manifest. Don't worry about success statistics, just operate in obedience, and do not doubt. You should not be focused on results!

James 1:6

"But let him ask in faith, with no doubting, for he who doubts is like a wave of the sea driven and tossed by the wind."

When you do see an immediate manifestation, be sure to give Jesus all the credit, taking none for yourself. Minister to the healed person, telling them what just happened, and how it happened. Offer the non-believer a chance to accept Jesus as Lord and Savior, and let the believers know that they can and should be walking in this same power. Finally, encourage the healed to attend a Bible believing church, and to learn more about the benefits of being a child of God. Advise them of any upcoming Spiritual First Responder meetings taking place in your area, as well.

It probably goes without saying, but you are to render your services for free, not expecting any compensation or fame for yourself when ministering healing. Freely you have received, freely you must give. There are plenty of well known personalities out there that are fleecing the flock, selling miracles. Never let yourself fall into this trap!

In summary, there are literally thousands of people waiting to be ministered to. The opportunities are limitless. There is nothing too big for God, as He has already provided healing for all diseases, and redemption of all sins.

Here are more scriptures for your reference:

Matthew 12:15

"But when Jesus knew it, He withdrew from there. And great multitudes followed Him, and He healed them all."

Matthew 10:7-8

"And as you go, preach, saying, 'The Kingdom of Heaven is at hand.' Heal the sick, cleanse the lepers, raise the dead, cast out demons. Freely you have received, freely give."

Mark 8:23-25

"So He took the blind man by the hand and led him out of town. And when He had spit on his eyes and put His hands on him, He asked him if he saw anything. And he looked up and said, 'I see men like trees walking.' Then He put His hands on his eyes again and made him look up. And he was restored and saw everything."

Luke 17:6

"So the Lord said, 'If you have faith as a mustard seed, you can say to this mulberry tree, be pulled up by the roots and be planted in the sea, and it would obey you.'"

Mark 11:23

"For assuredly I say to you, whoever says to this mountain, 'Be removed and be cast into the sea,' and does not doubt it in his heart, but believes that those things he says will be done, he will have whatever he says."

Matthew 10:1

"And when He had called His twelve disciples to Him, He gave them power over unclean spirits, to cast them out, and to heal all kinds of sickness and all kinds of disease."

1 Thessalonians 5:18

"In everything give thanks; for this is the will of God in Christ Jesus for you."

Include your favorite scriptures here:

Chapter 9

Healing Techniques

After you thoroughly understand the principles outlined in the previous chapters, and after you are confident in your spiritual identity, it is time to put into practice the material you have studied. Faith without works is dead, so it is time to get to work. You are now ready to heal the sick.

Here is the opportunity you have been waiting for, to actually see miracles happen right before your very eyes. You believe what the Bible says about healing; you know that Jesus has commanded you to lay hands on the sick. You, confident in your spiritual identity, are ready to exercise your Believer's Authority and begin your ministry. But, where and how do you start? How exactly are you supposed to bring about this healing?

If you are waiting on God to come down from Heaven and put up a billboard telling you it is time to get started, you will be waiting a long, long time. If you are waiting on a word from Jesus about getting started, or working with a particular individual, you should know that He has already given you the go-ahead in the Bible, which is full of His words for you. You don't need a sign, a word, or a feeling, as these all are meant to appeal to your emotions, or in other words, your soul. Just do what your spirit is telling you to do, go and heal the sick.

The world is full of sick and hurting people, ready to be ministered to. If you are experiencing fear, or worry about approaching these people, you are listening to the emotions of your soul, and not your spirit. Your spirit knows the truth, that you can do all things through Christ, who gives you the strength you need. Your spirit has the mind of Christ, and wants to see healing take place. Draw strength from your spirit, renew your mind and tell your body to take action by approaching those who need healing. God has not given us the spirit of fear, so be bold. You will be glad you did. Suppress any thoughts of doubt, and fear. Ignore them.

Actually, you will learn that people love to talk about their physical ailments. This ranks right up there with the weather and sports. Most people know plenty about what is wrong with them, so initiating a conversation with them should be fairly easy. A word of caution though, it is not necessary to know every detail about a person's medical background. Having too much information only serves to make the mountain you are moving seem bigger. Obviously you are not the one that has to move the mountain, as the Jesus within your spirit does all the heavy lifting for you. It is best for you to mentally step aside, so to speak, and let the Holy Spirit speak through you in helping to assess the situation. Again, avoid medical discussions if possible.

As a Spiritual First Responder, our goal is to quickly evaluate the situation, offer our services as a minister, and then move in the Believer's Authority to come against anything that would seek to be causing the problem. Over time, you will develop a smooth technique useful for approaching people. Your confidence will be high, and your faith will be high if you work at this often enough. At some point, the spirit inside of you will want to pray for every sick person you see. Do not be intimidated, simply be obedient. Once you see these miracles begin to manifest, you will want to do this for people as much as you can. Above all, be confident, but don't be pushy or overbearing.

Be especially gentle when you work with children, or the elderly. Your mission is to help, not hinder.

It bears repeating here that you are not a doctor, so do not, under any circumstance, try to practice medicine! Never, ever recommend that a person discontinue, or start, a medication. Doctors are great at making a diagnosis that you can use to help defeat the enemy. We are not against doctors, or anyone in the medical profession. Also, even though you are ministering, it is not the time for deep theological discussions, or arguments. You know the Word. Demonstrate it through the power of healing, and let that settle any issues regarding the benefits of knowing Jesus. The Spiritual First Responder gets the job done, and then you can make a recommendation about receiving Jesus, or attending a Bible believing church.

Exercising the Believer's Authority accompanied by the laying on of hands is probably the most productive method used for Divine healing today. This is the methodology we will discuss. It is important to remember that you are to avoid getting trapped into formulas, or worse, traditions of men. Encourage yourself to listen to the Holy Spirit, and let Him guide you when ministering healing. You will be amazed at what you see, and what you learn through your ministry. You will soon learn what works best for you, but remember to be open to adaptation should the need arise.

Before we get into the actual mechanics of ministering healing, it is important to note that the Bible dispels the teaching that it takes great faith or a special anointing to heal the sick. In fact, Jesus said that faith the size of a mustard seed can move a mountain:

Matthew 17:20

"I say to you, if you have faith as a mustard seed, you will say to this mountain, 'Move from here to there,' and it will move; and nothing will be impossible for you."

So, if it doesn't take great faith, what does it take? The answer is simple, it takes belief. We know this because Jesus told His disciples, earlier in that same verse, that they were experiencing trouble because of their unbelief.

Matthew 17:20

"So Jesus said to them, 'Because of your unbelief.'"

They presumed it to be a lack of faith on their part, but Jesus immediately cleared it up by telling them that even the smallest amount of faith works, but unbelief had thwarted their efforts.

Faith is essential on your part; simply have faith to believe what you have studied. The faith that it does take, is a supernatural, God-given faith that dwells in your spirit. It was placed there by Jesus the instant you accepted His salvation. There is human faith, and there is Heavenly faith. Human faith comes from your soul, or mind, while Heavenly faith comes from your spirit. There is an obvious difference between the two. Human faith relies upon information delivered to you by your five senses. For example, you have faith that a chair will hold you up if you sit in it because your eyes tell you that it has four legs. Your hands can tell you if the chair is made of durable material. Yes, it takes faith to sit in the chair, but your actions are based on visible information coming from your body.

Heavenly faith asks you to believe in things you cannot touch, taste, smell, see, or hear. Heaven and Hell are two such things, as well as salvation and healing. It takes supernatural faith to believe in supernatural things. This supernatural faith dwells in our spirit, which has been made righteous through Christ Jesus.

Romans 3:22

"Even the righteousness of God which is by faith of Jesus Christ unto all and upon all them that believe: for there is no difference."

Notice that it does not say faith in Jesus, but faith of Jesus. You have the mind of Christ in your spirit. It is out of your spirit that you heal, and not out of your emotions, or soul. If it comes from your mind, you are trying to heal with your own power. If it comes from your spirit, you are using the power of Jesus, who indwells your spirit.

If you have compassion on the sick, that emanates from your spirit. If you have sympathy for the sick, that emanates from your soul. Sympathy is an emotional counterfeit of compassion. You must speak from the spirit, and this takes practice to get it right.

God will not tell you again to go and heal the sick. He has already commanded us do so in His Word. Don't be fooled into thinking that you need a sign to get started. This is one of Satan's favorite tactics, along with fear, which tries to delay your efforts, or talk you out of action altogether. Do not wait for special feelings, gut reactions, or impressions about approaching the sick. These may very well come, but do not wait around for them. If you do, you are listening to your soul, and ignoring what your spirit is telling you. Jesus wants to heal, now go make it happen.

Fear is of Satan. Boldness is of the Lord. You have the power of the Holy Spirit in you, therefore operate in boldness. Never be afraid to approach the sick and hurting.

Before you minister to someone, get their permission to do so. Most people will readily grant you permission to help them. However, if someone rejects your offer outright, simply give them your contact information and let them know you were concerned, and thought you could help. If you have to beg someone, it will likely inhibit your chances for success. Some people actually want to hold on to their diseases, though hard to believe. Many people find their identity in their ailments; it becomes who they are, their story. Some derive their income from being sick. At most, ask at least once more, and lean on the Holy Spirit to make the connection for you. It is not up to you to force anyone to be healed. Also, there is only one requirement on their part for a person to be healed; they must have the need to be healed. The Bible clearly states this in the Gospel of Luke.

Once permission has been granted, extend your hands and make contact with the person. Many Spiritual First Responders who are just starting out prefer to hold hands with the sick person. As you develop your techniques, feel free to place your hand on, or near the part of the body that is having symptoms. Here, we must stress common sense is to be employed, along with modesty. Be very alert for any indication that your sick person might have an aversion to being touched; it can happen. Respect their wishes, and please stay away from private or sensitive areas of the body. You can ask them to put their hand near the affected area, and then with their permission place your hand on top of theirs. Again, your goal is to make contact with them allowing the healing power to flow from your spirit into their body.

In the Bible, Jesus commanded a fig tree to die, and it did from the roots up. His disciples were amazed at this, and wanted to know more. Jesus began to teach them a lesson about faith, and belief. He told them that they can move mountains with their faith, if they believe it in their hearts. This amazing demonstration of power translates into our ministries today. There is no recorded place in the Bible where Jesus prays for the sick. He used His authority to do the job. Peter's mother-in-law was in bed with a fever. Jesus spoke directly to the fever, rebuking it and commanding it to leave. The fever left her immediately. There are many instances in the New Testament that give an account of Jesus healing through His authority. Take time to research the techniques Jesus used, and remember that He still performs these miracles today through you.

As we have already learned, Jesus gave us permission to use the authority of His name when we lay hands on the sick. After you have made contact with your sick person, it is time to express your Believer's Authority and see these miracles take place. Encourage the person to relax and let God do the healing; don't let them try to be healed. Forbid them to pray as you begin to minister to them. You are trying to pour into them, and it makes it harder when they are pouring out their prayers while you are ministering. It takes absolutely no faith on their part to be healed. In the course of your ministry, you likely will see atheists healed as well as believers.

When you begin to speak, do not pray for God to heal the person in front of you. Do not beg Him to move on behalf of this person, or in any way suggest that He should do what He has commanded you to do. He told you to heal the sick. Reflect back on your training and know and believe that Jesus has already paid the price for this. He bore our sicknesses, so there is no need for anyone to be sick, thanks to His sacrifice. In your mind, work up a sincere, righteous anger for the devil who has brought this sickness upon this person. Understand your mission is to deliver Jesus into their body through the power of the Holy Spirit, driving out anything that seeks to cause them disease or pain.

Using your Believer's Authority, begin to speak to the mountain. If it is pain, address it by name and tell it to leave in the name of Jesus. Speak with determination, from your spirit, not your emotions. This takes some practice, but you will soon be able to distinguish the difference. If you are dealing with a disease process, such as cancer, speak directly to it commanding it to die and leave in the name of Jesus. This is not merely idle chatter. At this point you have invoked the supernatural forces of Almighty God on your behalf. Again, speak from your spirit, raising your voice if necessary. This is spiritual warfare; you are to destroy the works of the enemy!

Feel free to command body parts to move back into place; for organs to be repaired or replaced. There is nothing too big for God at this point, and you will likely be amazed at what you begin to see happening. Start commanding blind eyes to open, and deaf ears to hear in the name of Jesus. Some miracles take more time to manifest than others, just be patient and keep after it. Heal knees, backs, shortened legs or arms, emotional issues, and muscular problems. Do it all in the name of Jesus, remembering to give Him thanks once the process has started or is complete.

Let's look at a few possible real-world scenarios, beginning with approaching an obviously sick person.

Here is a sample script useful in initiating a conversation with them:

"I noticed your cane, what happened to you?" "Are you in any pain at the moment?" "I am a minister, and I believe that prayer will make this feel better. Would you mind if I whispered a little prayer for you right now?"

This small script will undoubtedly open up many opportunities for you to minister to the sick. It allows you to greet the person, assess the situation, and minister to the person. If they grant you permission, they will be grateful that someone cared enough to notice.

You are now a Spiritual First Responder. Your awareness is keen; you are on a mission from God. You will be pleasantly surprised at the Divine appointments that will be dropped into your lap. You will be in line at the grocery store and someone in front of you will start complaining of a migraine headache. You know how to handle it, so let them know you can help. You do not need to be overly religious to do this, just be yourself. Possibly someone at your office will talk of being depressed. You have what they need, and it is not long counseling sessions. The power of God can heal mental issues as quickly as physical problems. Do not get bogged down in the list of symptoms, concentrate on delivering the cure.

Once your recipient has declared a problem, it is time for you to go into action. Here is what to do, preferably in this order:

Get some basic details about the disease or sickness; particularly find out if the disease has a name. Remember, the name of Jesus is above all others.

Philippians 2:9-10

"Therefore God also has highly exalted Him and given Him the name which is above every name, that at the name of Jesus every knee shall bow, of those in Heaven, and those on Earth, and of those under the Earth."

If applicable, ask if there is any pain associated with the ailment. Pain is a great indicator of the effectiveness of your prayer. If the pain lessens, you know you are on the right track. If it moves from one place in the body to another, this is indicative of pain caused by a spirit of infirmity. If you can get it to move, you can get it to leave.

Now that you have made an initial assessment of the situation, ask for permission to pray.

Tell the person to relax, while explaining the process of laying on of hands. It is helpful to let the person know that your belief in this process comes from the instructions Jesus gave to us in the last chapter of Mark. At this point, the person should know what to expect, and be ready for you minister to them. If there is any uncertainty, this is the time to clarify your intentions.

Mark 16:17-18

"And these things will follow those who believe: In My name they will cast out demons, they will speak with new tongues, they will take up serpents; and if they drink anything deadly, it will by no means hurt them; they will lay hands on the sick, and they will recover."

Sometimes it is helpful to let the person direct your hand to the part of their body which is experiencing the discomfort. If it is a generalized disease such as fibromyalgia, place your hands in theirs. Many Spiritual First Responders do this consistently, but getting closer to the source of trouble can be helpful in certain situations.

Once positioned, it is now time to deliver the power of God, straight out of your spirit. Here is a sample script for use with someone being attacked by cancer:

"In the name of Jesus Christ, and by the power of the Holy Spirit, I bind the spirit of cancer. Cancer, you must bow at the mighty name of Jesus, and I curse you now, and speak death unto you right down to your very root and seed. I bind you, and I order you to leave this dear child of God, NOW, in the name of Jesus. Cancer, go NOW!"

This is not a fast rule or formula that must be followed, simply a suggestion which shows you how the Believer's Authority is put into action. A special emphasis is put on the word "now" to indicate that this comes from your spirit. You have to convince the disease that you mean business, and you are aware of the power of the name of Jesus. Speaking this word loudly, or forcibly, tends to ensure that it emanates from your spirit, rather than your mind.

Feel free to command the body to repair itself of any damage caused by the disease, and speak restoration into their body, as well as encouragement. Here is a follow-up declaration:

"I order this body to repair all the damage caused by cancer, and in the name of Jesus I speak full restoration into you. I speak life and light into you right now in the name of Jesus. Any spirit of death, any spirit of fear, and any other spirit of infirmity, I bind you and order you to leave NOW. I speak peace into you in the name of Jesus. Thank you Jesus for your healing."

When you are working with pain, speak directly to it using your Believer's Authority. Here is a practical example of dealing with someone experiencing a sprained ankle:

"In the name of Jesus, I command every muscle, every tendon, every nerve, and bone in this ankle to line up right now with the perfect Word and will of Jesus Christ. I speak total restoration into this ankle, and in the name of Jesus, pain you go NOW! In the name of Jesus, pain you leave NOW."

At this point, you can have the person test out the ankle or any other body part by flexing it. This is sometimes known as testing their faith to see the results of your prayer. If they report a reduction in pain, you can beat it altogether. Here is how you would follow up in this case:

"Jesus, we thank you for your healing touch, and know that you are a God of one-hundred percent. Now, in the name of Jesus, ankle I command you to be healed. Pain, go NOW. Pain, you must go in the name of Jesus!"

Have the person check it again, and likely you will have been successful in your mission as a Spiritual First Responder.

Again, these examples are not formulas you must adhere to. Sometimes, keeping it simple is the best option. Many people are instantly healed with a single word, such as "LIFE" spoken forcefully from your spirit. Simply release the Kingdom of God into the person and let the Holy Spirit sort it out. Avoid trying to tell Him what needs to be done by using too many words. Though hard to believe, making things too complicated can actually hinder your results. Trust in the fact that Holy Spirit knows more about the situation than you do!

Be confident in knowing that you have enacted the supernatural to move on your behalf. If you do not see an immediate manifestation, assure the sick person that you are believing for their one-hundred percent recovery. Often, a person's healing will manifest at night while sleeping, when they have disengaged their minds, freeing their body up to be healed. The mind is powerful, and it can get in the way. This is why you should ask the person to relax as much as possible. Never pull your faith back by saying it did not work; it is working the minute the command left your lips. We are to be obedient, letting Jesus sort out the details. The more you practice this, the better your results will be. Once you start seeing miracles it really promotes confidence in Jesus and the promises to us in the Word of God.

After you minister, offer some brief follow-up information, perhaps even suggesting a good Bible believing church. Avoiding long theological discussions, it is now time to try to find out if the person has a relationship with Jesus. If they do not, feel free to share the Gospel with them. There will never be a better time.

On a quick note, avoid trying to triage people based on your perception of their problems. Don't let someone in a wheelchair intimidate you; pray for them. It is just as easy for God to raise them up as it is for Him to heal a headache. It takes no more or less faith on your part, simply belief in what Jesus has already accomplished.

It would be impossible to cover all examples of techniques in this manual. You simply must get out there and put this teaching into action. The Holy Spirit will guide you through the process.

Sickness and disease are often caused by demons. We are commanded to cast them out of people. Occasionally, you will see a demon manifest and begin speaking through the individual you are ministering to. They do not want to leave, but in the name of Jesus, they must. Do not chat with demons, as they are all liars anyway. This is counterproductive and serves no purpose. Keep ordering the demon to leave, relying on the authority of the name of Jesus. It has to go, and it will. This process is known as deliverance. Most demons will readily leave and provide no confrontation. Do not be scared if a demon manifests in the course of your ministry, be prepared.

We are commanded to raise people from the dead. Though it sounds impossible, it can and does happen. If you run into a situation where someone has died, simply start commanding life and light into the person, rebuking the spirit of death, all in the name of Jesus. Speak to their body just as if it were alive, and don't be afraid to be persistent.

In these situations, you should be respectful to family members that are present. Do your best, and use common sense as these awkward situations can be quite stressful.

Sometimes when people are prayed for, they will fall out under the power of God. Do not be alarmed if this happens, but do not be caught off guard either. A person that falls can take you down with them, or even get hurt in the process. Be aware of your surroundings. If you believe this might be a possibility, take appropriate action by having someone with you that can help catch, or soften a fall. Remember, you are to help them, not hurt them!

Getting with a group of trained Spiritual First Responders is a great way to enhance your faith and build your confidence. Jesus had disciples, and they learned to do this by His example. He never taught them to do this, they watched and learned. Once you learn to heal the sick, pass along the information to others, by example, and let them get in on the blessings, as well. Even a person who has just become a believer can immediately heal the sick. There is no need to wait for any special anointing to get started.

In summary, if you have been properly trained, healing the sick is easy. The Jesus in you is still healing today, if you let Him. Exercise the Believer's Authority He gave you to cast out demons, to heal the sick, and even to raise the dead.

Here are some additional scriptures for your review:

James 2:26

"For as the body without the spirit is dead, so faith without works is dead also."

2 Timothy 1:7

"For God has not given us a spirit of fear, but of power and of love and of a sound mind."

Philippians 4:13

"I can do all things through Christ who strengthens me."

Ephesians 6:12

"For we do not wrestle against flesh and blood, but against principalities, against powers, against the rulers of the darkness of this age, against spiritual hosts of wickedness in the heavenly places."

Mark 11:13-14

"And seeing from afar a fig tree having leaves, He went to see if perhaps He would find something on it. When He came to it, He found nothing but leaves, for it was not the season for figs. In response, Jesus said to it,' Let no one eat fruit from you ever again.' And His disciples heard it."

John 8:32

"And you shall know the truth, and the truth shall make you free."

Luke 4:39

"So He stood over her and rebuked the fever, and it left her. And immediately she arose and served them."

Luke 8:54-55

"But He put them all outside, took her by the hand and called, saying, 'Little girl, arise.' Then her spirit returned, and she arose immediately. He commanded that she be given something to eat."

Mark 3:11

"And the unclean spirits, whenever they saw Him, fell down before Him and cried out, saying 'You are the Son of God.'"

Luke 9:11

"But when the multitudes knew it, they followed Him; and He received them and spoke to them about the Kingdom of God, and healed those who had need of healing."

Mark 11:23

"For assuredly I say to you, whoever says to this mountain, 'Be removed and be cast into the sea,' and does not doubt it in his heart, but believes that those things he says will be done, he will have whatever he says."

Include your favorite scriptures here:

Chapter 10

Maintaining Your Healing

So now that you have put into practice the techniques you have learned, what happens after you see a healing miracle manifest? Knowing how to follow up is important, and will certainly help to keep the people you minister to remaining happy and healthy.

Many of the miracles you see will happen instantly, while others will take time to manifest. As you already know, many illnesses are caused by demonic spirits, which in the course of healing, are made to leave the person you are ministering to. It is not beyond the mission of a demon to try and come back to see if the host will allow it to return.

When this happens, original symptoms may try to reappear, leading the person to believe that their healing did not work. When you think about this, you can readily see how confusing this could be. Therefore, informing healed people about this potential phenomenon will help them to deal with the doubts these demons are able to instill. You must guard against disbelief, at all costs, as it can rob them of their healing.

First and foremost, credit for the healing must be given to Jesus Christ, who paid the price for it. Most people will know they have been healed the minute it happens. The pain will disappear, movement will return to a restricted joint or limb, sight or hearing will return, and other manifestations will make it perfectly clear that something has happened. Help the person you are ministering to come to this conclusion by doing something that previously was a challenge to them. Get them to confess their healing, and lead them in a prayer that thanks Jesus for making it possible. Make sure they understand that you are simply acting in obedience to the Lord, and it was not of your own ability that the miracle transpired.

If you believe the person's problem was indeed caused by a spirit of infirmity, it is crucial to instruct him or her on what to do if any symptom tries to return. Satan can go to work on these people and try to convince them they were not healed. When the first hint of pain tries to come back, instruct the person to reclaim the fact they were indeed healed by Jesus, and to rebuke the symptom. If they remain determined, and continue to rebuke the symptom in the name of Jesus, it will eventually subside. Yes, the devil will go away and not return. In effect, you are instilling the Believer's Authority within them and teaching them how to exercise it.

The Bible says that when a demon is cast out, it will return to see if its host will allow it back in.

Matthew 12:43-45

"When an unclean spirit goes out of a man, he goes through dry places, seeking rest, and finds none. Then he says, 'I will return to my house from which I came.' And when he comes, he finds it empty, swept, and put in order. Then he goes and takes with him seven other spirits more wicked than himself, and they enter and dwell there; and the last state of that man is worse than the first. So shall it also be with this wicked generation."

It is important to fill the void with the Holy Spirit, guarding the mind with the Word of God. This is a spiritual battle.

Knowledge is power. Informing people that these spirits might make an attempt at this will be helpful. It is not your place to instill fear, but to convey information. If you are filled with Jesus, there is no need to be worried about these issues. Go forth in confidence, the battle is already won.

James 4:7

"Therefore submit to God. Resist the devil and he will flee from you."

Obviously there is nothing wrong with adhering to healthy lifestyle habits. However, making a doctrine out of this, as some people do, serves to take the focus off of Jesus. It is because of Him that we have health, and not of our own doing.

1 Timothy 4:8

"For bodily exercise profits a little, but godliness is profitable for all things, having promise of the life that now is and of that which is to come."

Disease is not brought on by God, it is caused by the consequences of sin, or by a direct attack from Satan. If you have continuous sin in your life, the devil will use this as an open door to attack you. For example, if you are prone to abusing alcohol, it can seriously affect your liver. Jesus can instantly heal your liver, but returning to alcoholism invites the devil to attack you again. We must strive to avoid sin because our bodies are the temple of the Holy Spirit.

Finally, avoid going to places that reinforce the old traditions of men. Stay away from churches that try to add to the Word of God. If you go back to what caused you trouble in the first place, you are asking for trouble again. Avoid these situations at all costs; your health depends on it. If you attend a church that teaches that healing is not for today, you will likely find yourself sick again for sitting under this false teaching.

Walking in Divine health is the key to maintaining your health and eliminating the need for Divine healing. The goal is to not have to suffer through the attacks of illness that Satan attempts to initially inflict upon us, and those we minister to. If you need to, lay hands on yourself and use your Believer's Authority to fight disease in your own body. Do not trust in how you feel, trust in what you know, by His stripes we were healed.

It is important that you teach people the secret of Divine health. Most churches ignore this concept, and fail to teach this scriptural truth. The people you minister to can easily come to the false conclusion that they need you to help them every time they are sick. Teaching Divine health is the best way to avoid this misconception. Although it is not possible to always have lengthy theological discussions after you minister a healing, just try to hit the main points so preparation can be made to help keep these people healthy. Try to get them involved in a spirit-filled church.

Your identity should be in Jesus, not in an illness or disease. Too often people get to know us by what challenges we are facing. At all costs, avoid broadcasting to others what you are facing. Though in the natural, it seems as if the more people there are that know about your problem, the better off you will be. This is not true, because it only breeds negative unbelief, and ineffective prayer from those not walking in the truth. Be careful what you say, speaking only positive affirmations about your healing. Life and death reside in the power of the tongue.

In summary, it is best to stay healthy by learning to use your Believer's Authority to ward off any attacks of the devil. Teaching others how to do this helps them hold on to the abundant life that Jesus has promised for us.

Here are some scriptures that will be of help to you in this area:

Matthew 28:18-19

"And Jesus spoke to them, saying, 'All authority has been given to me in Heaven and on Earth. Go therefore and make disciples of all nations, baptizing them in the name of the Father and of the Son and of the Holy Spirit.'"

John 10:10

"The thief does not come except to steal, and to kill, and to destroy. I have come that they may have life, and that they may have it more abundantly."

1 Corinthians 6:19-20

"Or do you not know that your body is the temple of the Holy Spirit who is in you, whom you have from God, and you are not your own? For you were bought at a price; therefore glorify God in your body and in your spirit, which are God's."

Proverbs 18:21

"Death and life are in the power of the tongue, and those who love it will eat its fruit."

Include your favorite scriptures here:

About the Author

Michael Politoski

Born in Texas, in 1959, Mike Politoski was raised in a Christian home that believed in the teachings of the Baptist Church. He attended a private Christian school in a small East Texas town, and later studied electronics technology in college.

Mike began his broadcasting career in 1977, and after a series of on-air jobs at a few radio stations in the Dallas–Fort Worth area, he became affiliated with Praise Broadcasting Network, a Christian radio ministry.

He has performed as a national television host, and now assists the staff of PBN with radio and television productions. Mike has a sincere desire to promote the Gospel through electronic media.

Married to his wife Letty, residing in North Carolina, he has been blessed with three children.

In 2011, Mike was diagnosed with cancer, and underwent surgery to remove it. His treatments included chemotherapy and radiation. He had been contributing to a small African American church in his community, but not attending their services. When they became aware of his hospitalization, they came to visit him, and prayed the prayer of faith over him. As a result of this, his prognosis came back excellent, and he has been healed. Since then, Mike regularly attends this church, and considers it home.

Inspired by what happened to him in the hospital, Mike began a quest to find out as much as possible about Divine Healing. He has spent thousands of hours researching techniques that work, and weeding out the ones that do not work. He has seen blind eyes opened, deaf ears hearing, and a wide assortment of other miracles, all happening through the name of Jesus.

He has committed his life to sharing with others the message of Jesus, teaching them how to lay hands on the sick and seeing them recover. Mike is already planning on releasing additional books in the future on this subject, so stay tuned!

If you desire to contact Mike for a speaking engagement at your church or other venue, or if you would like to share a healing testimony, you may reach him by email at:

mike@spiritualfirstresponders.com

He enjoys corresponding with other believers who are interested in Divine Healing.

Notes

Notes